SUPERCAR
COLORING BOOK

Belongs to:

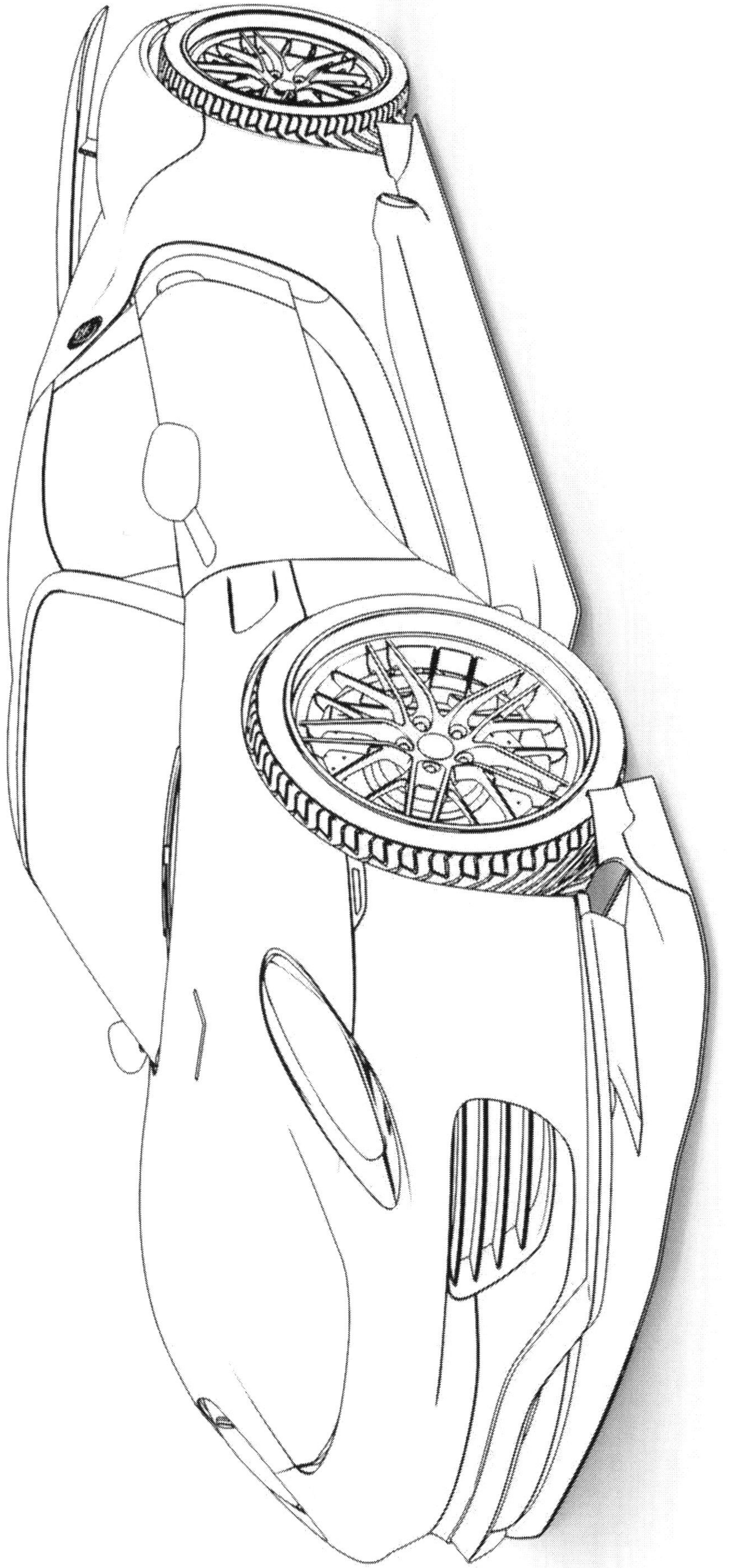

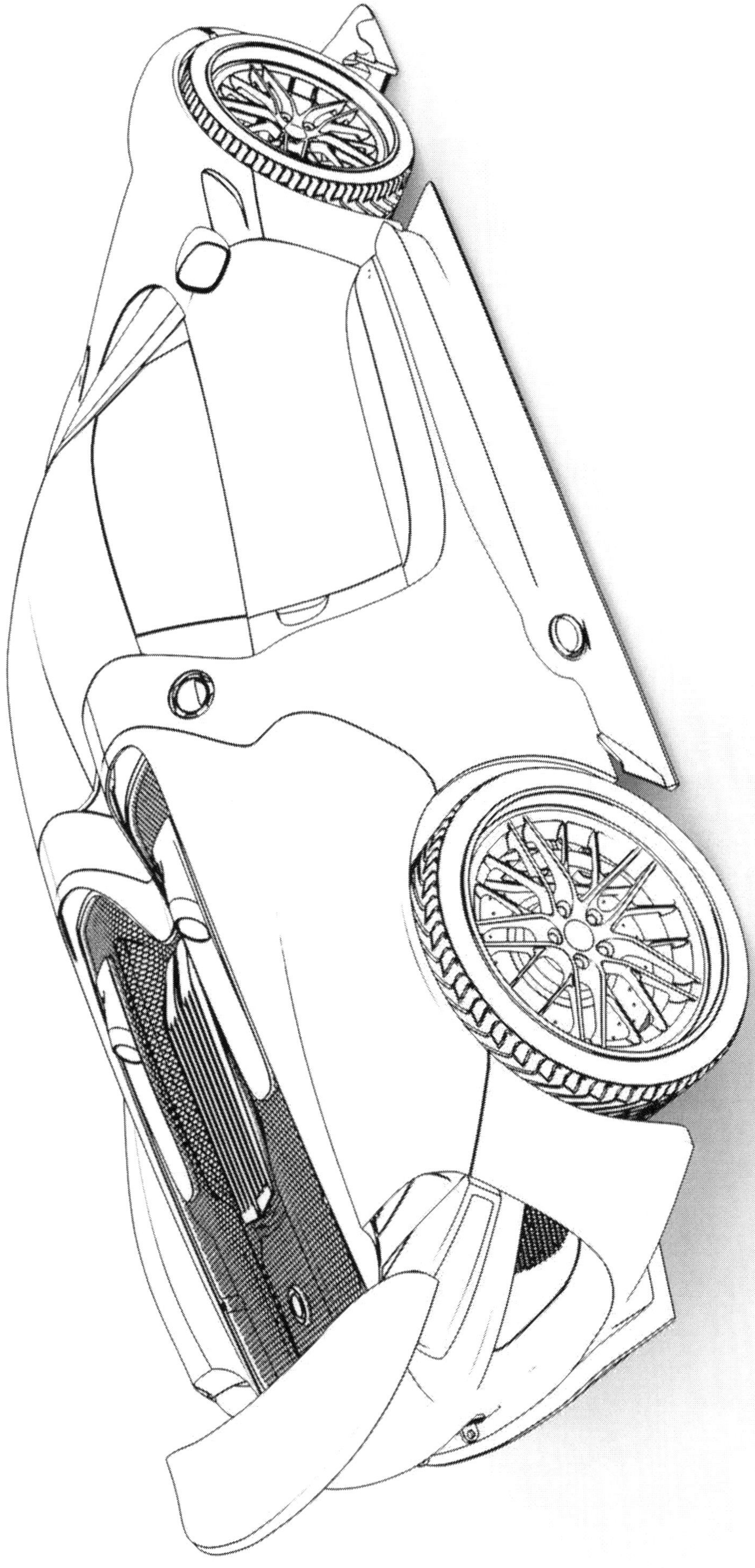

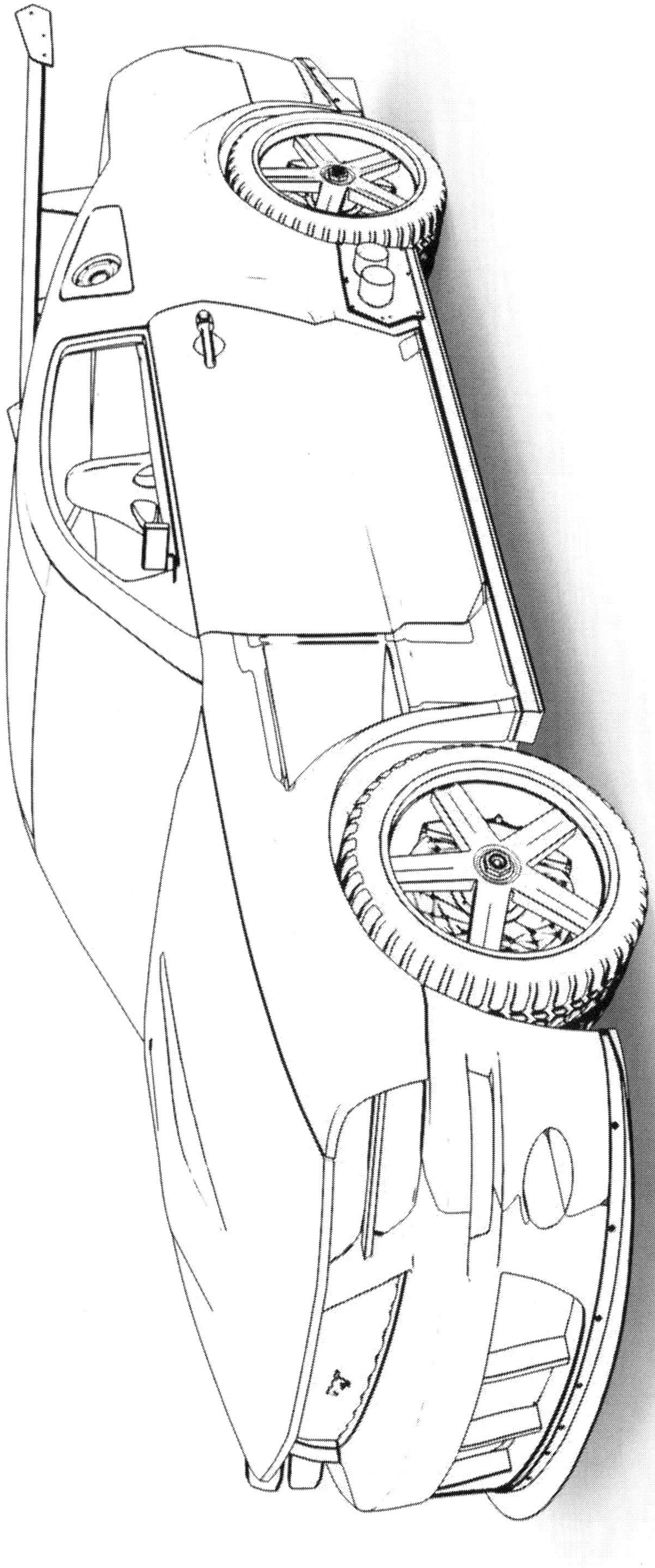

Firebird

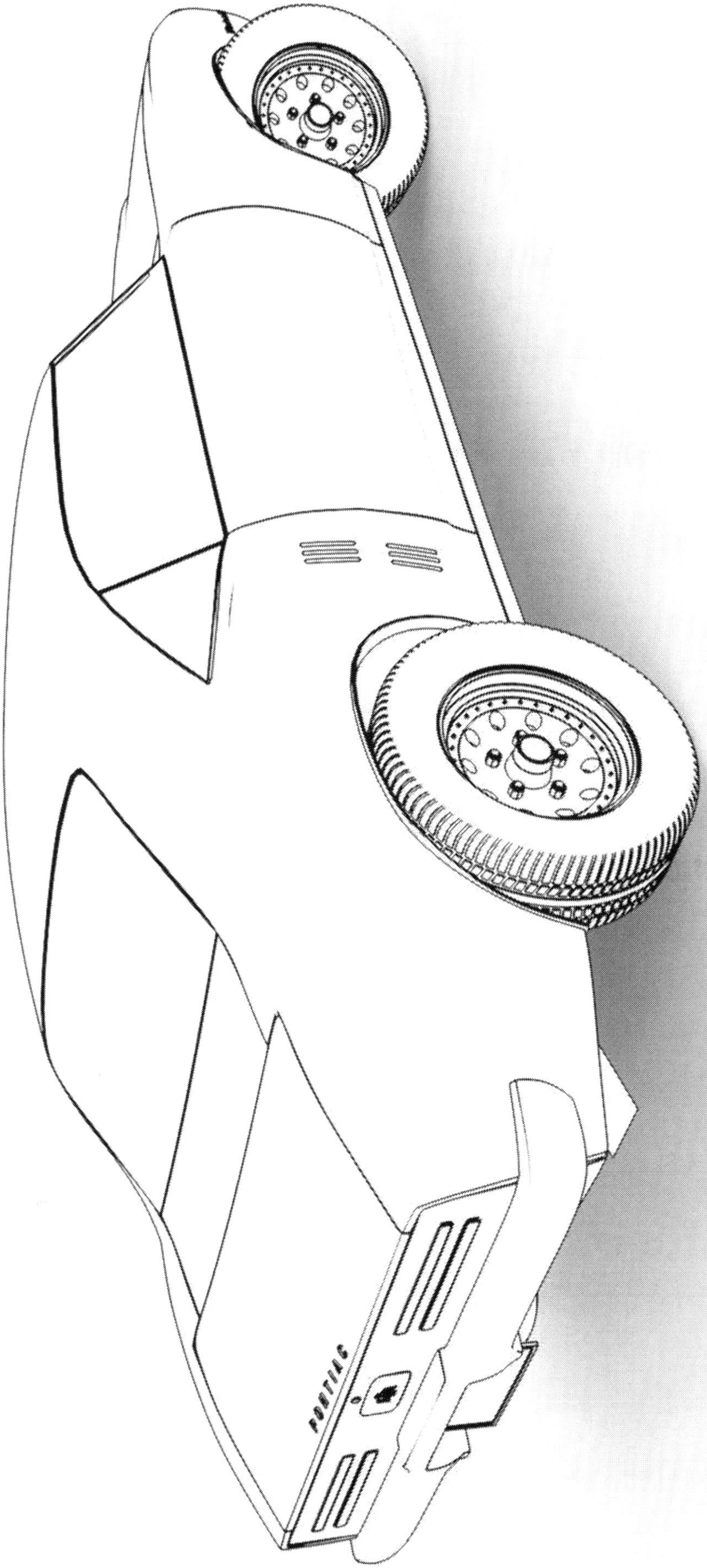
PONTIAC

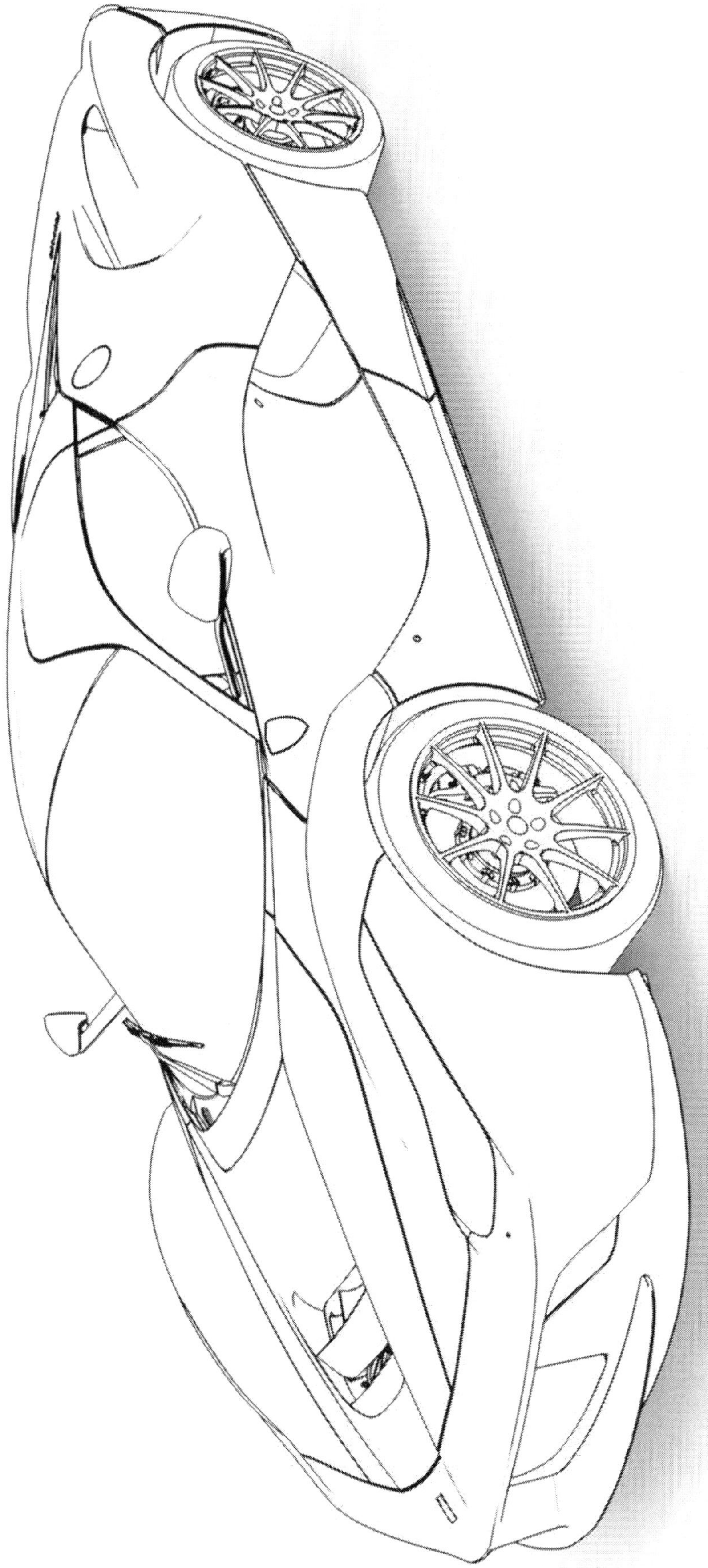

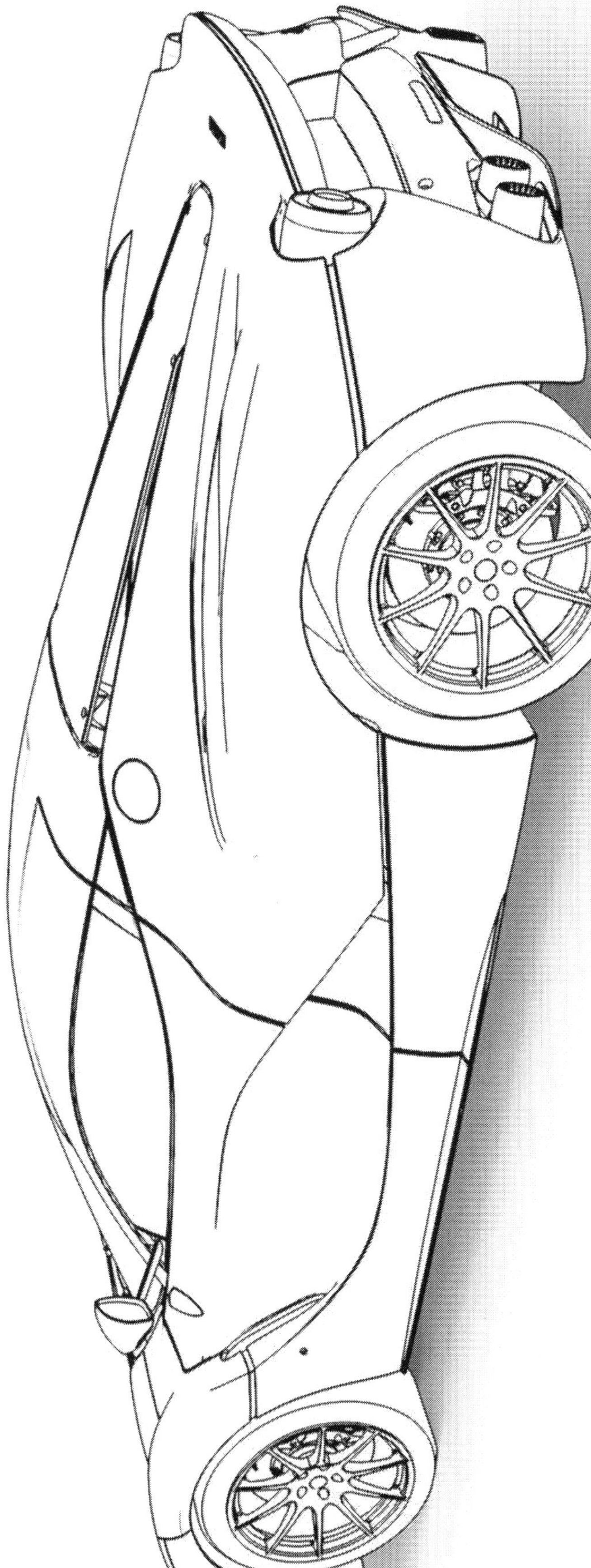

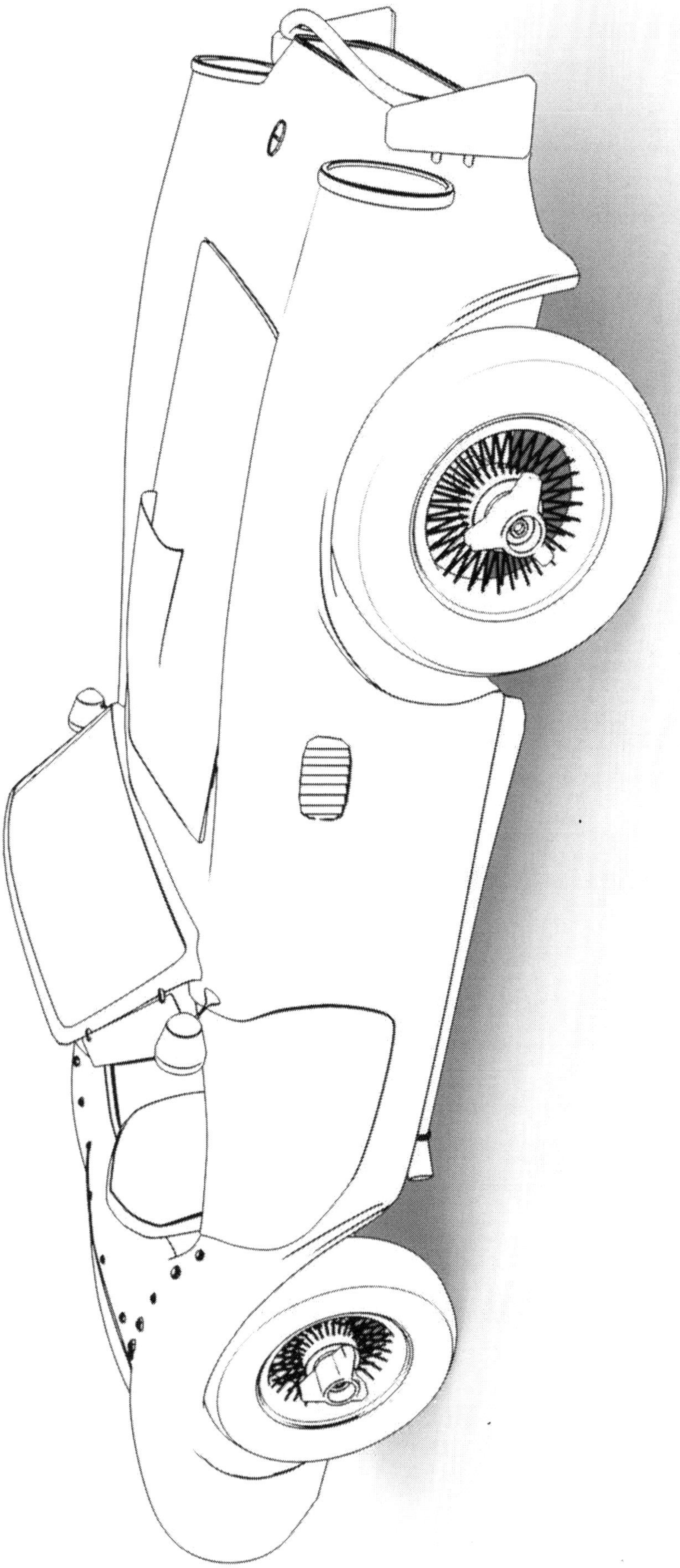

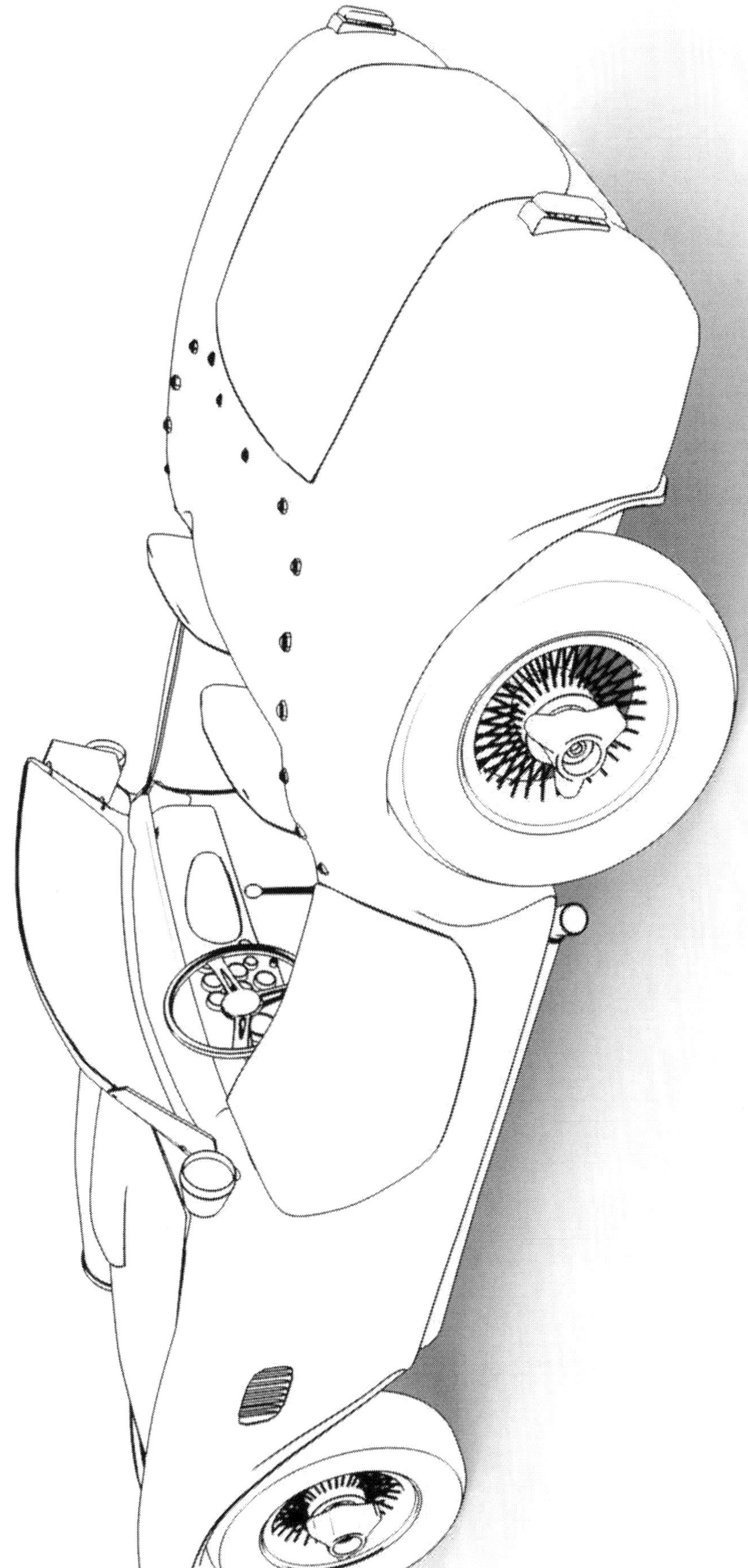

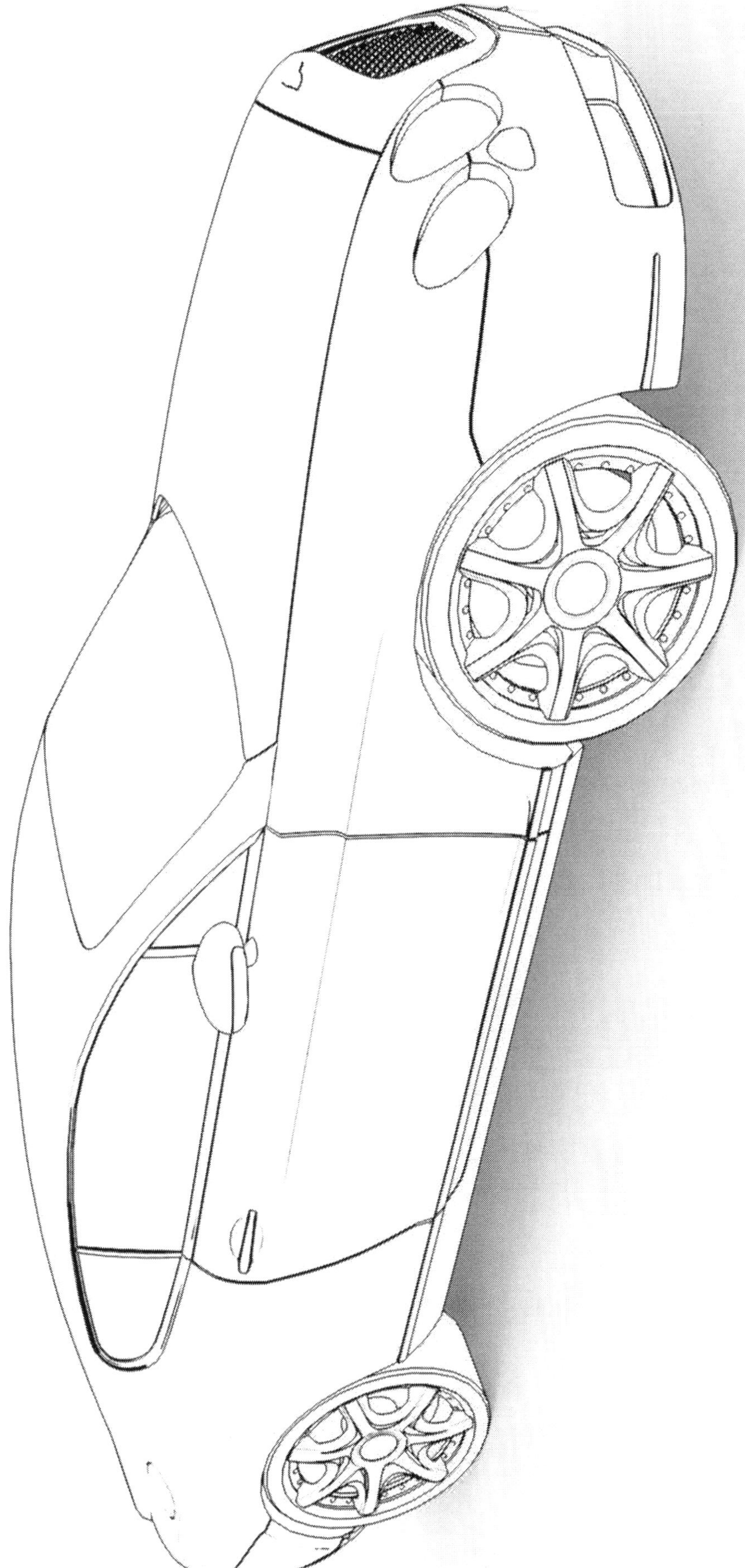

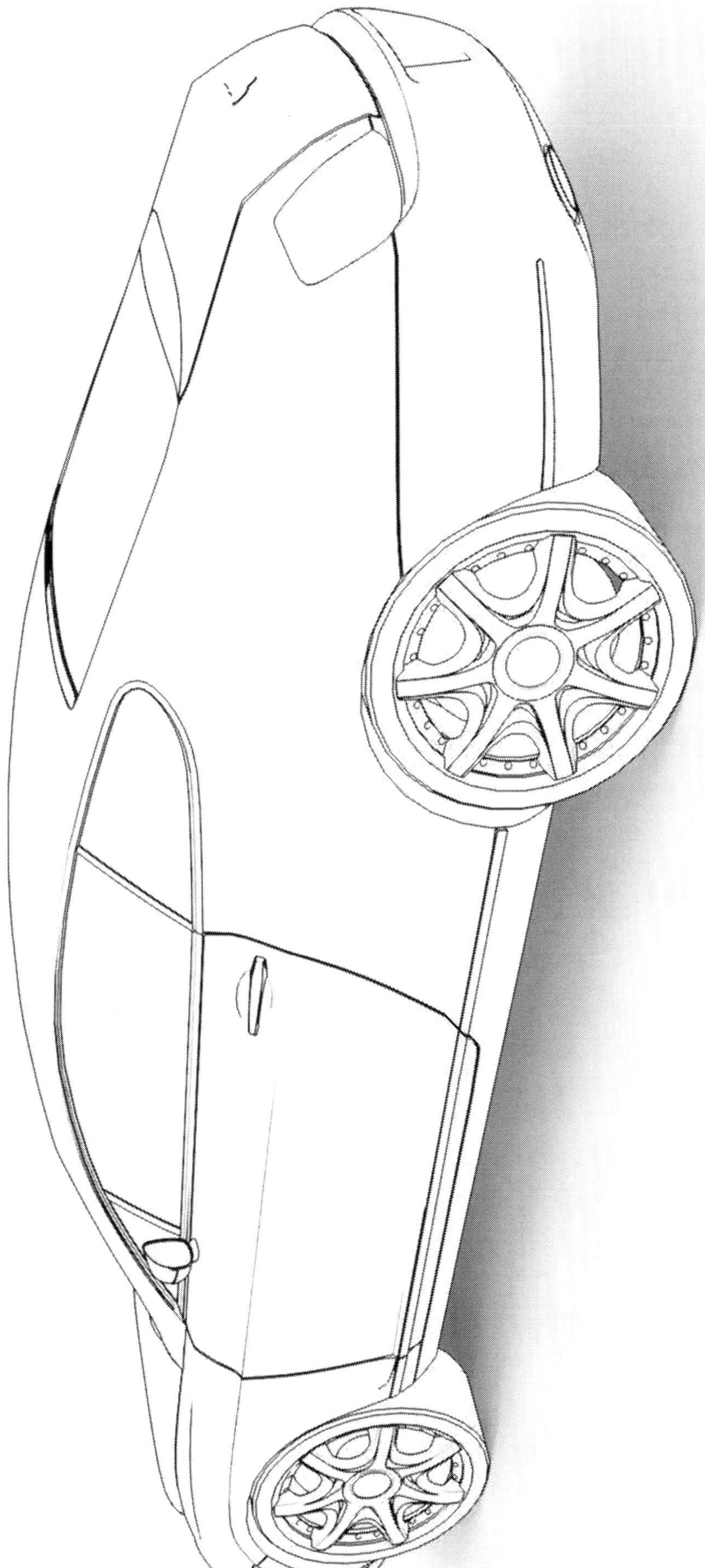

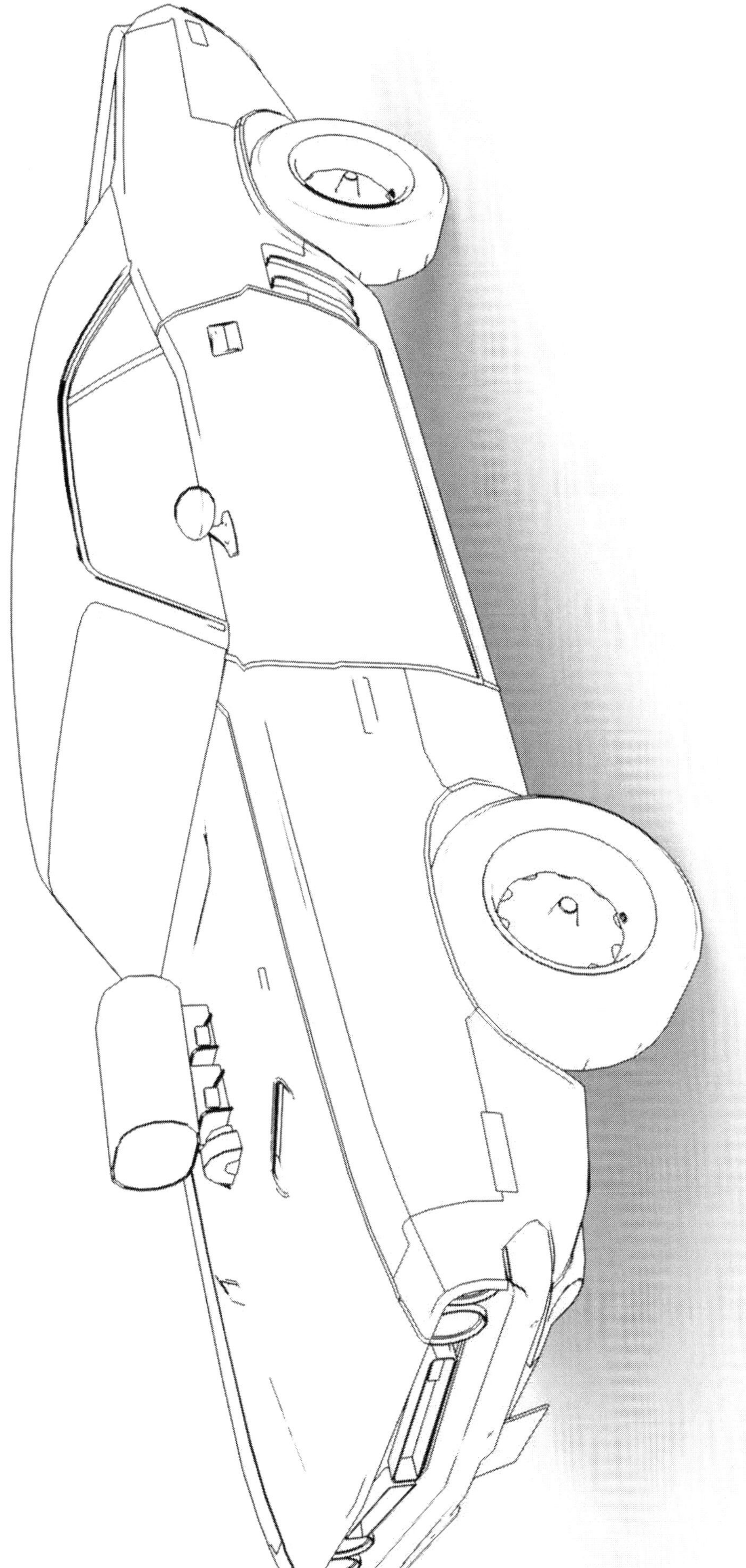

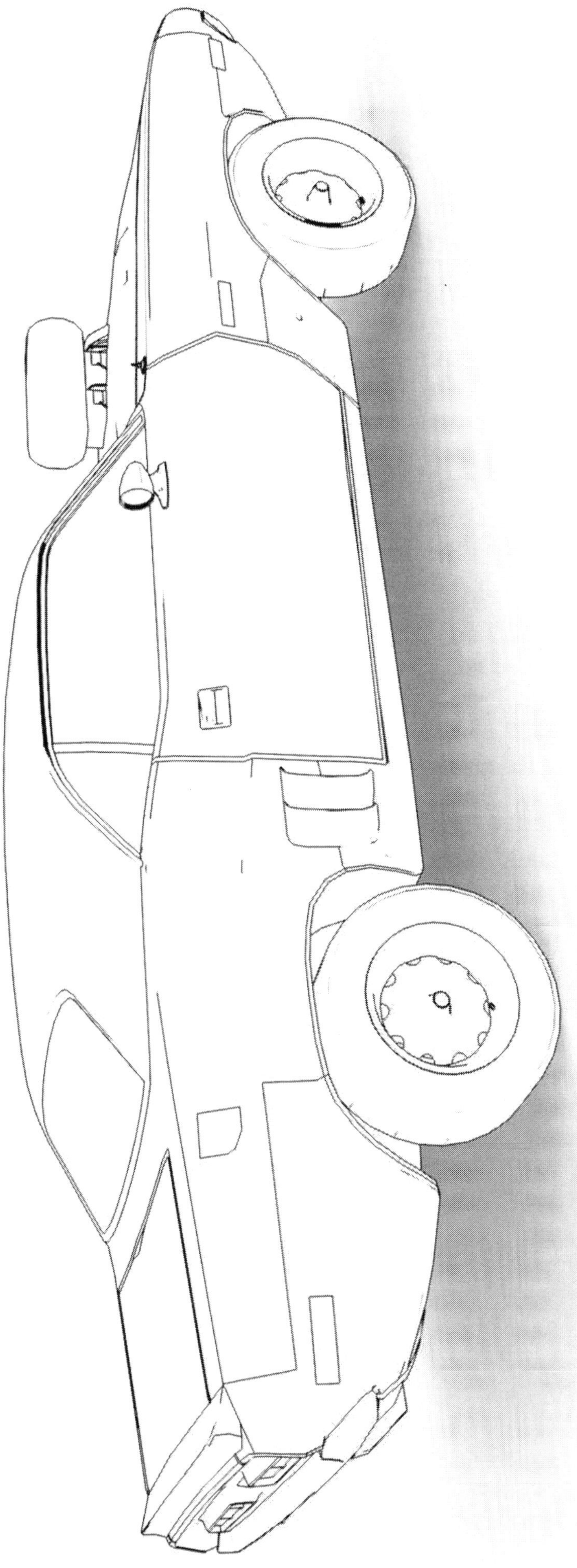

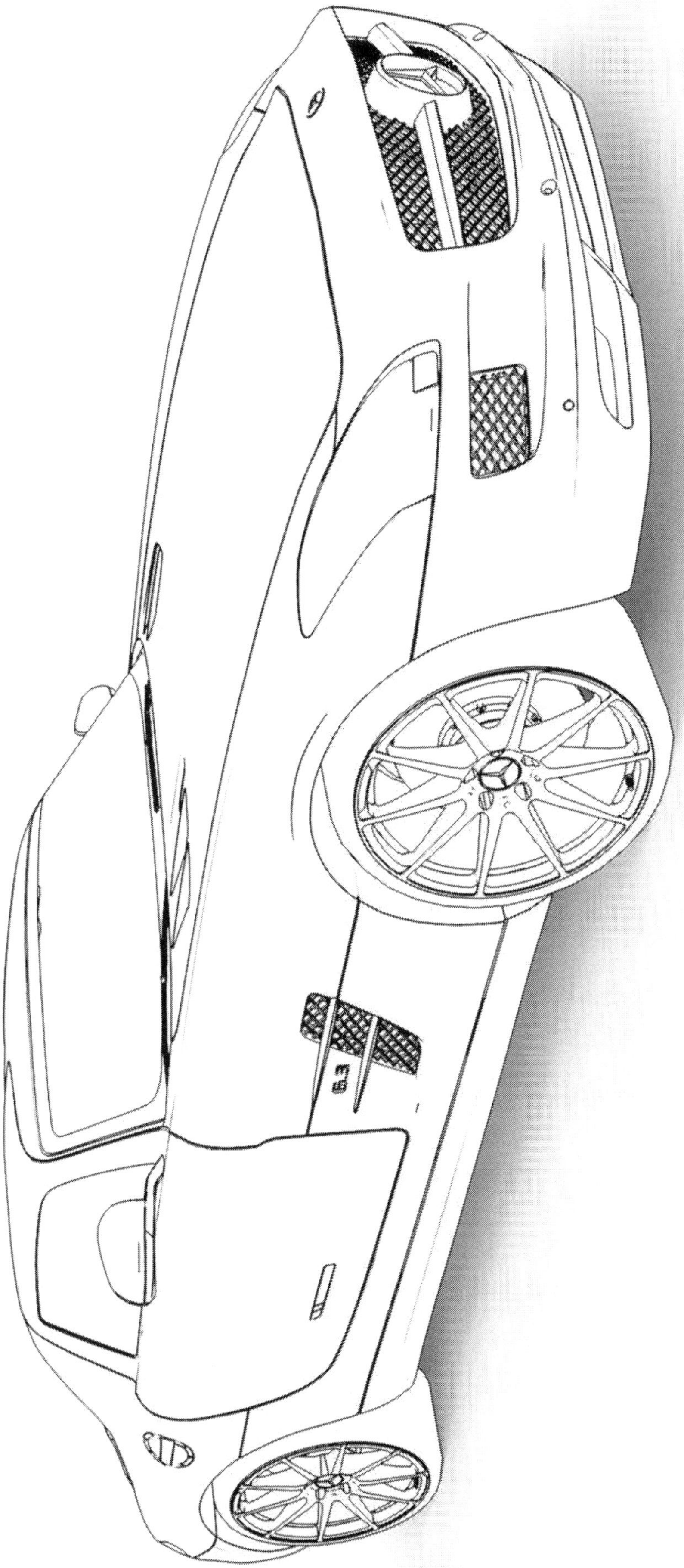
6.3

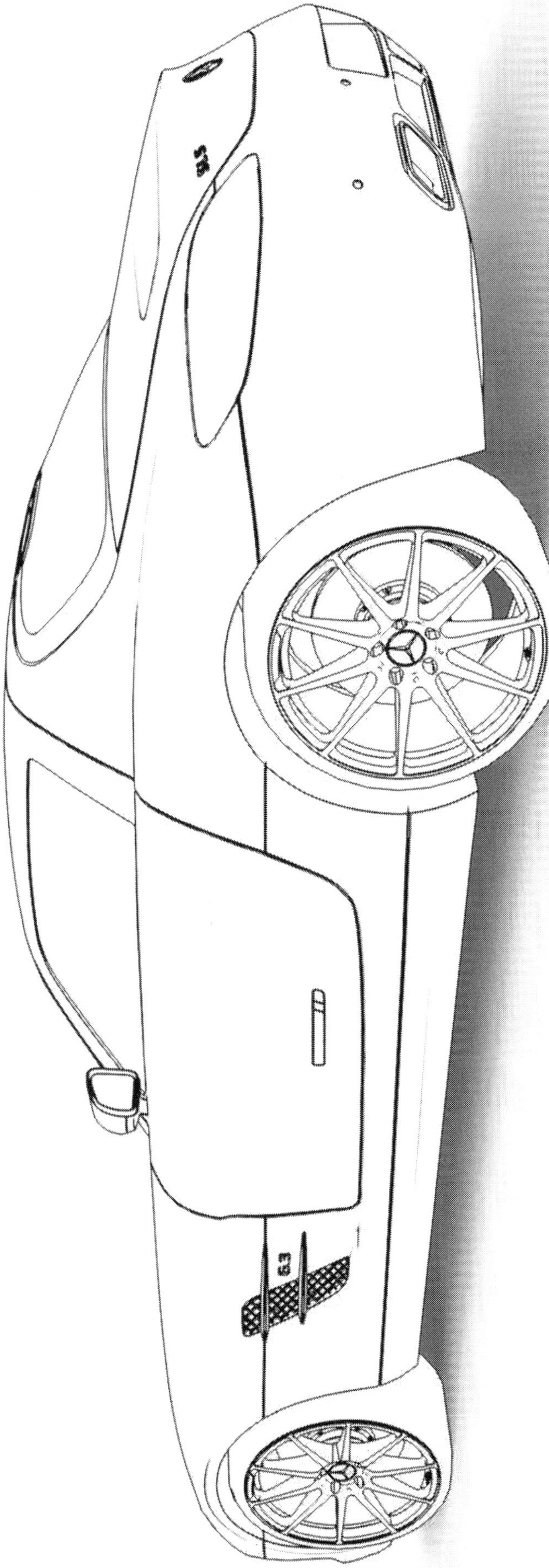
6.3

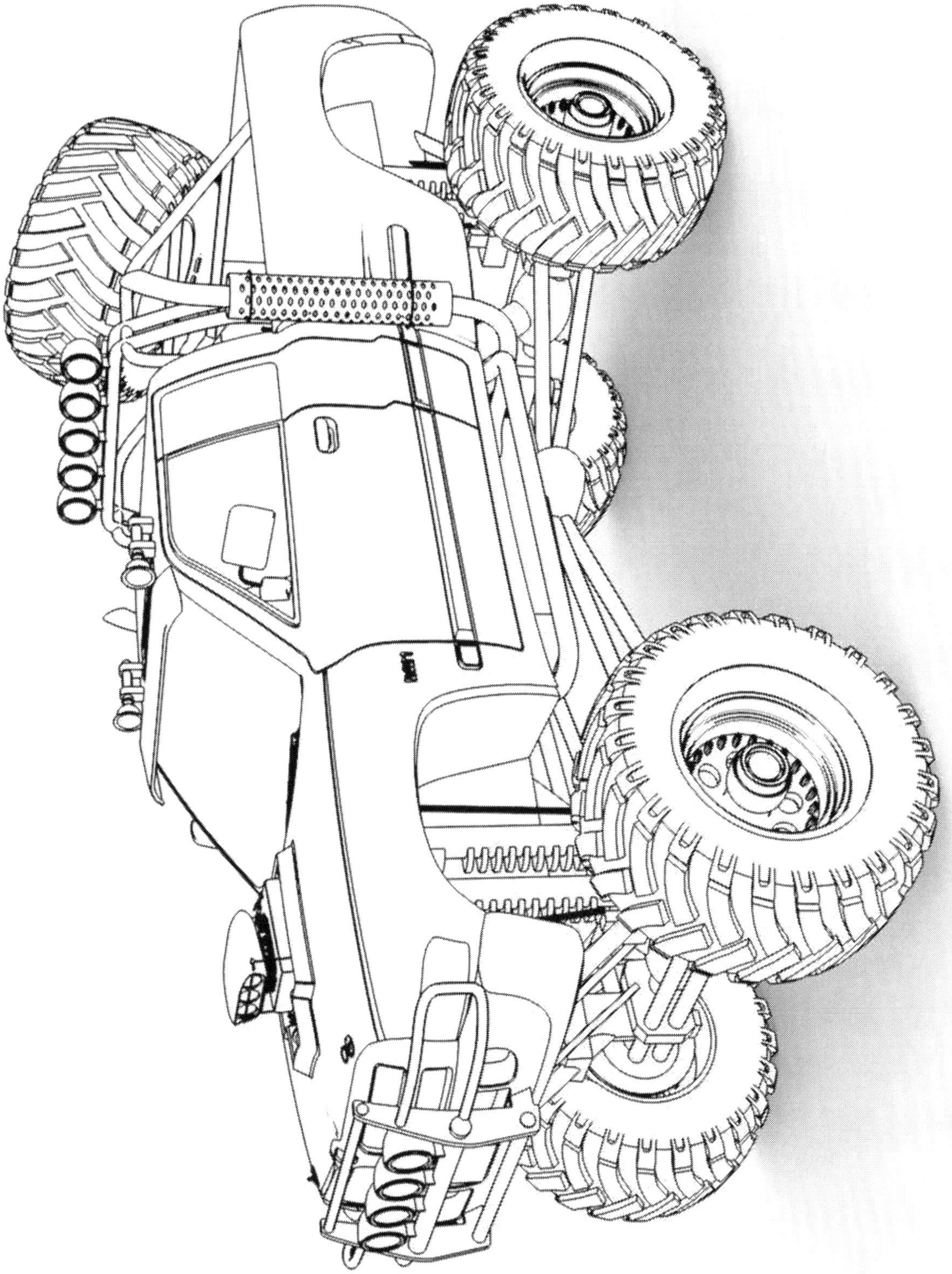

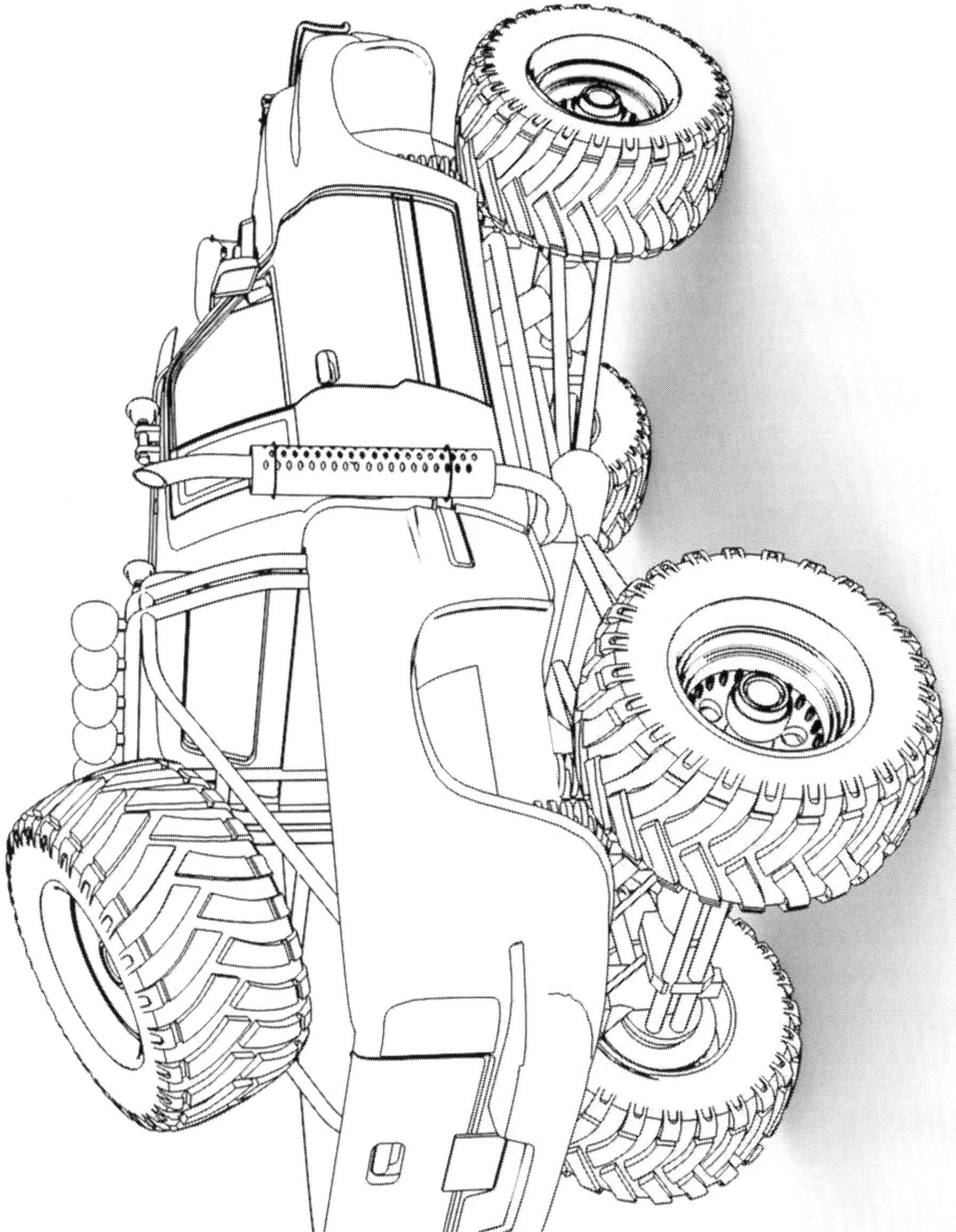

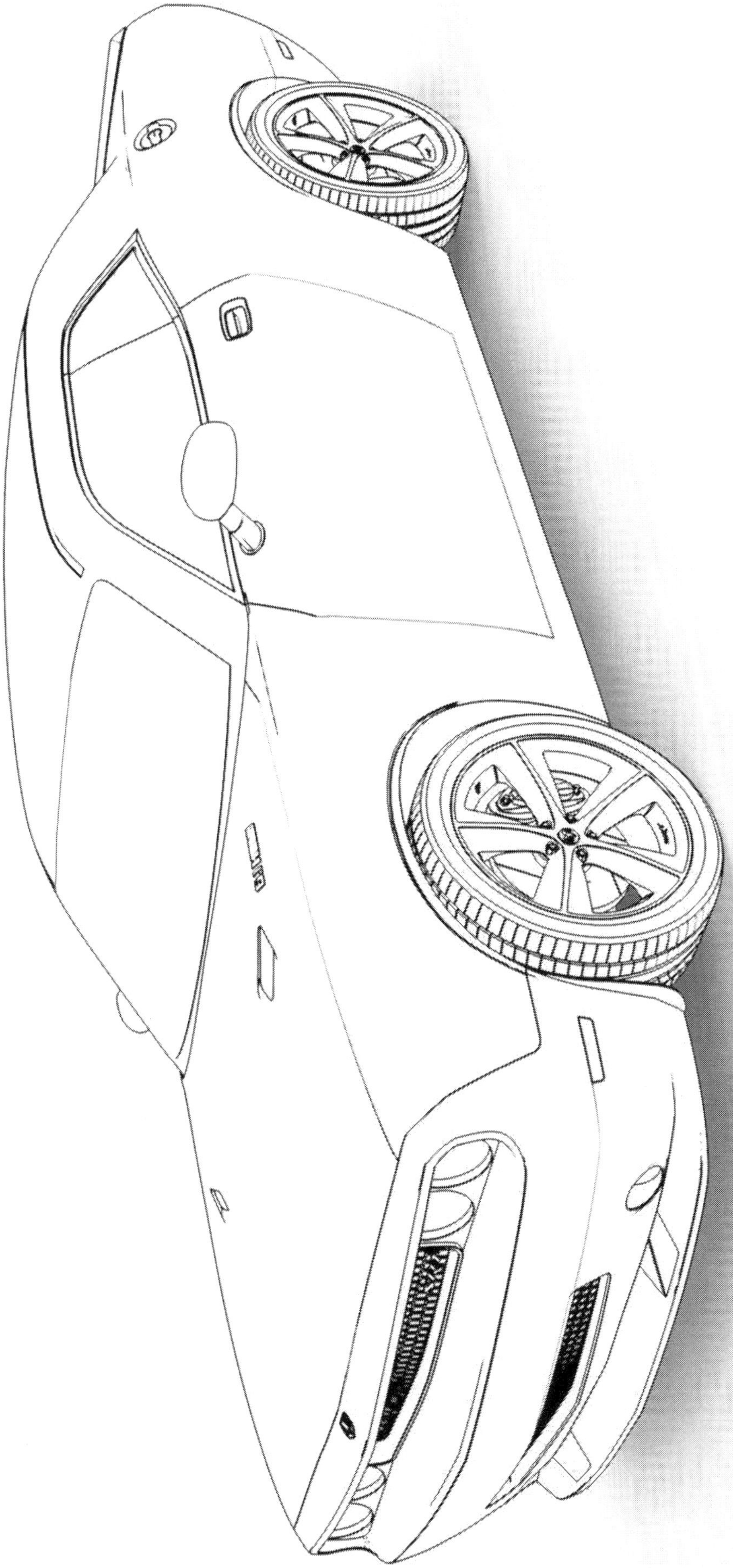

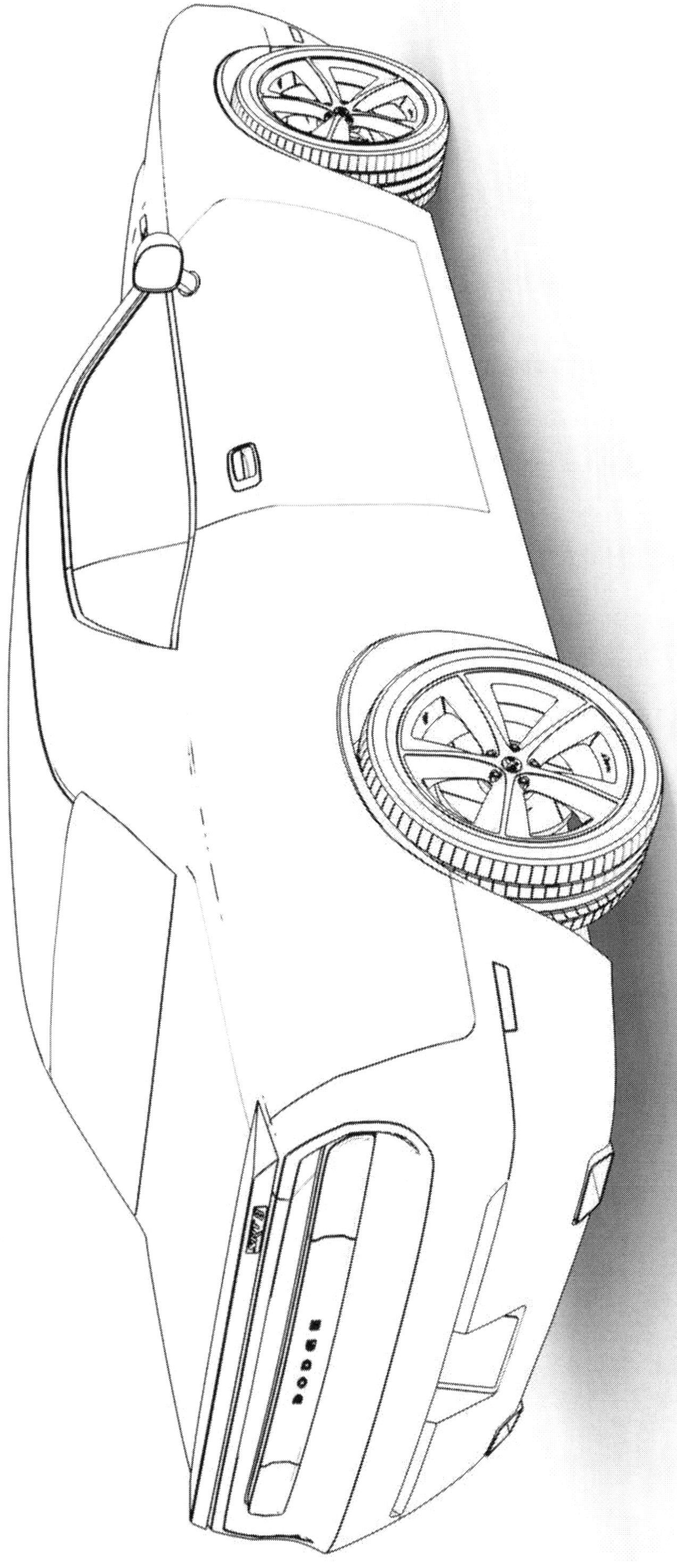

V8

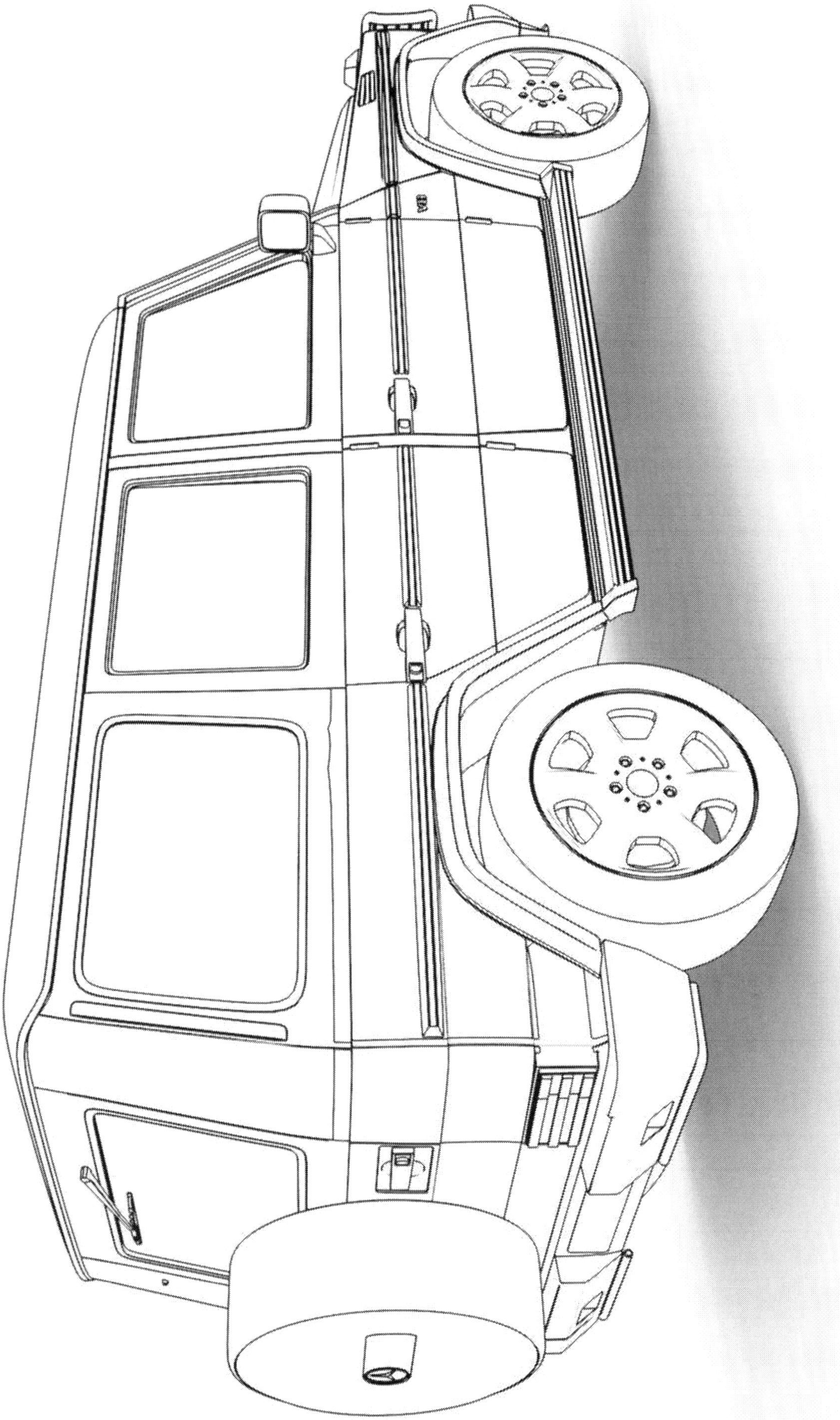

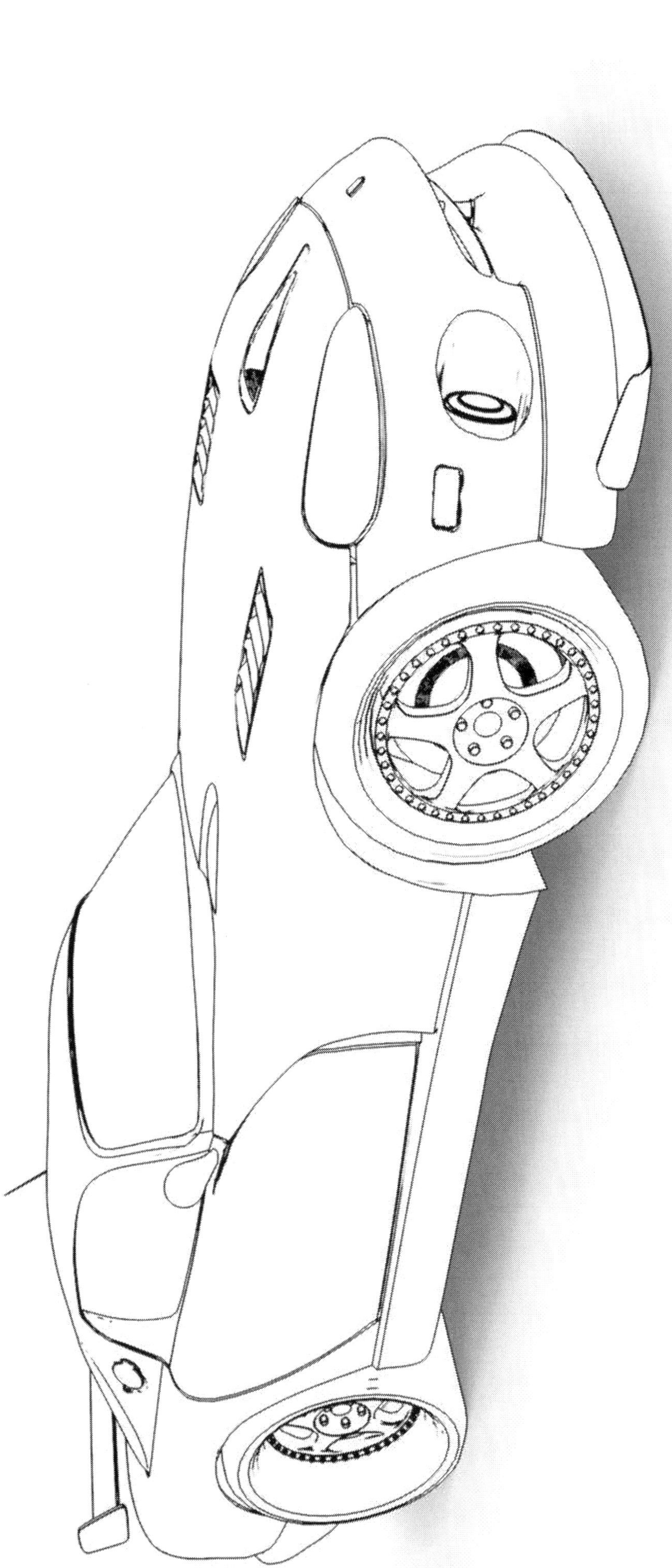

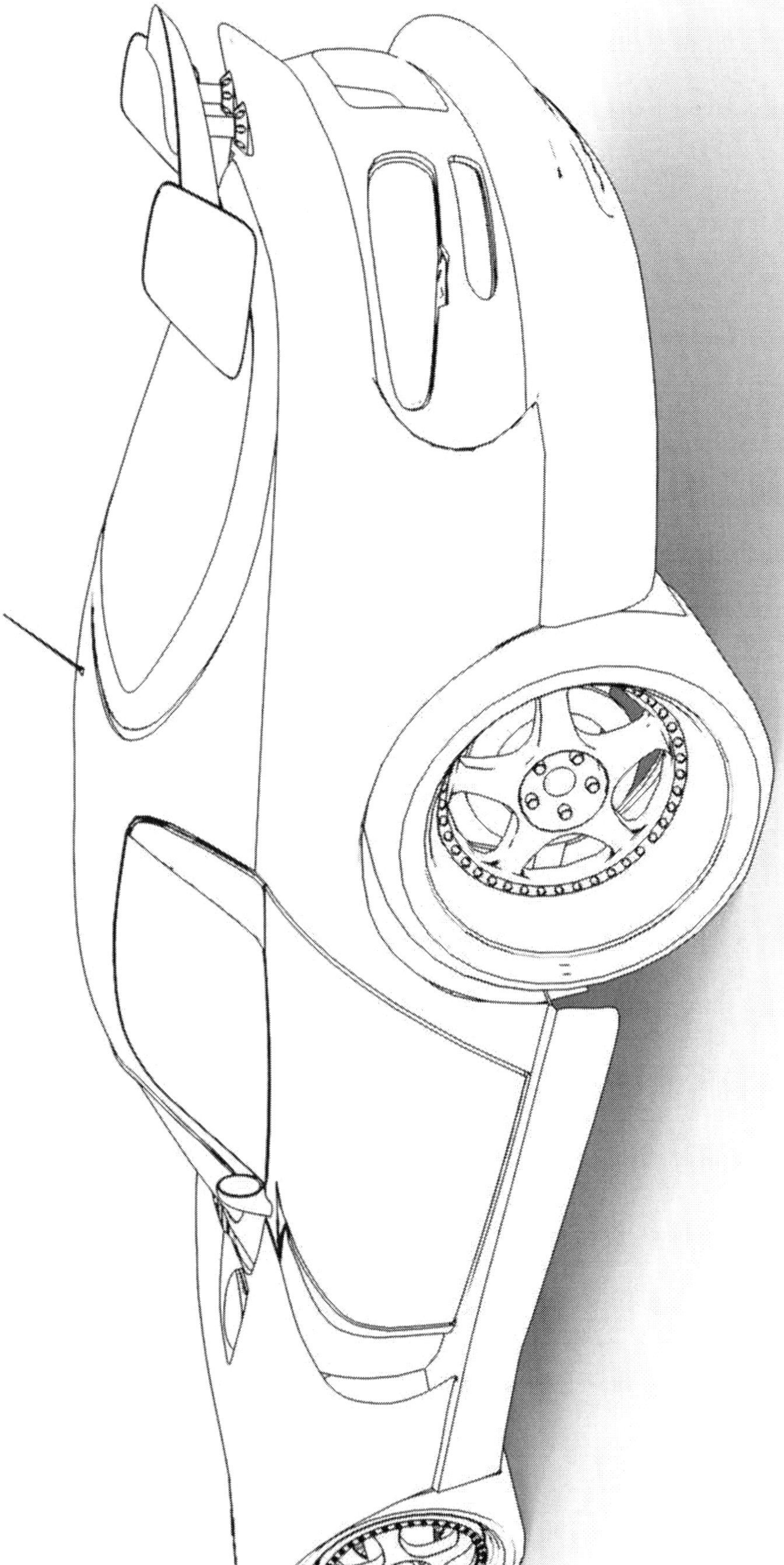

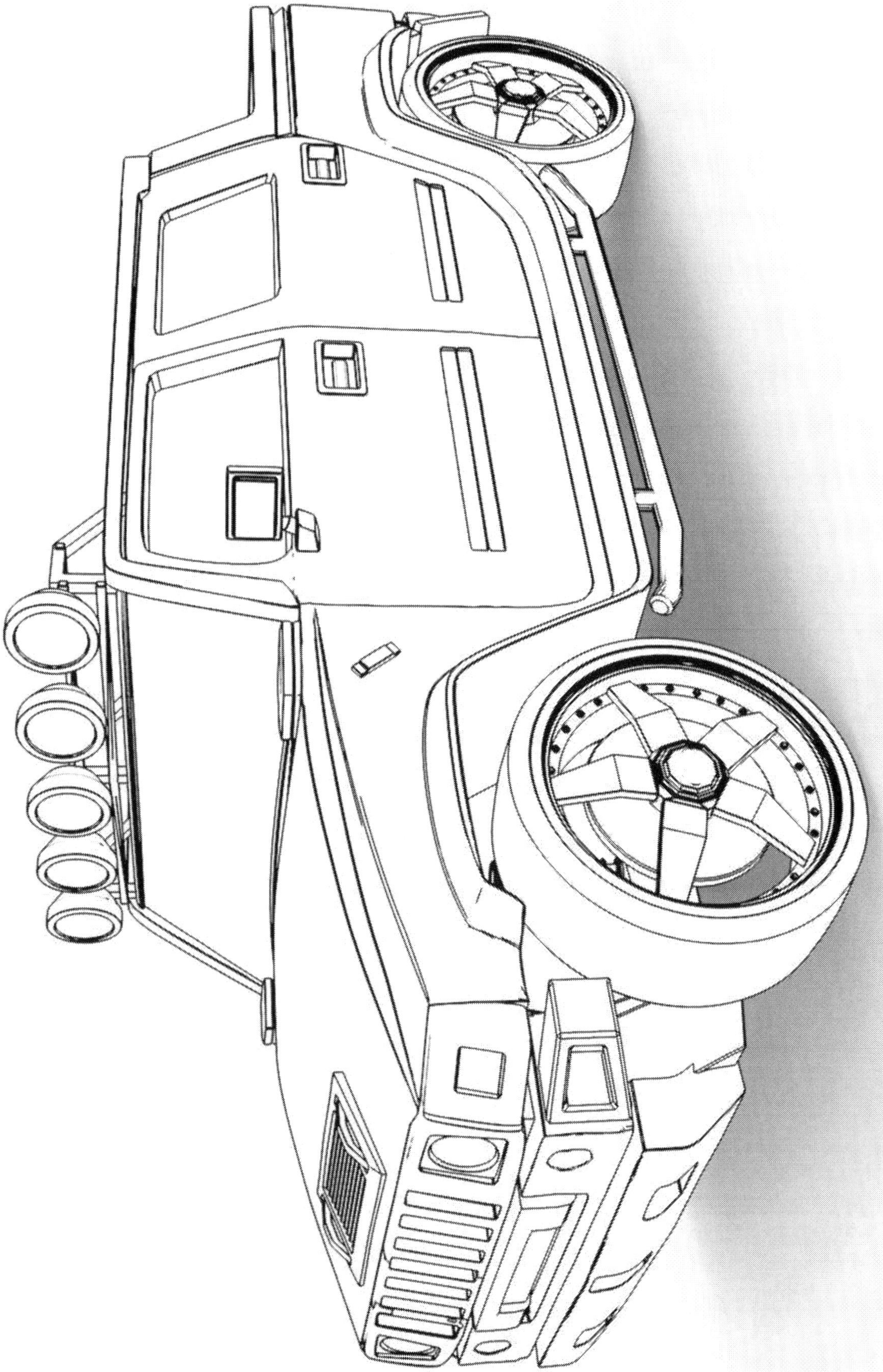

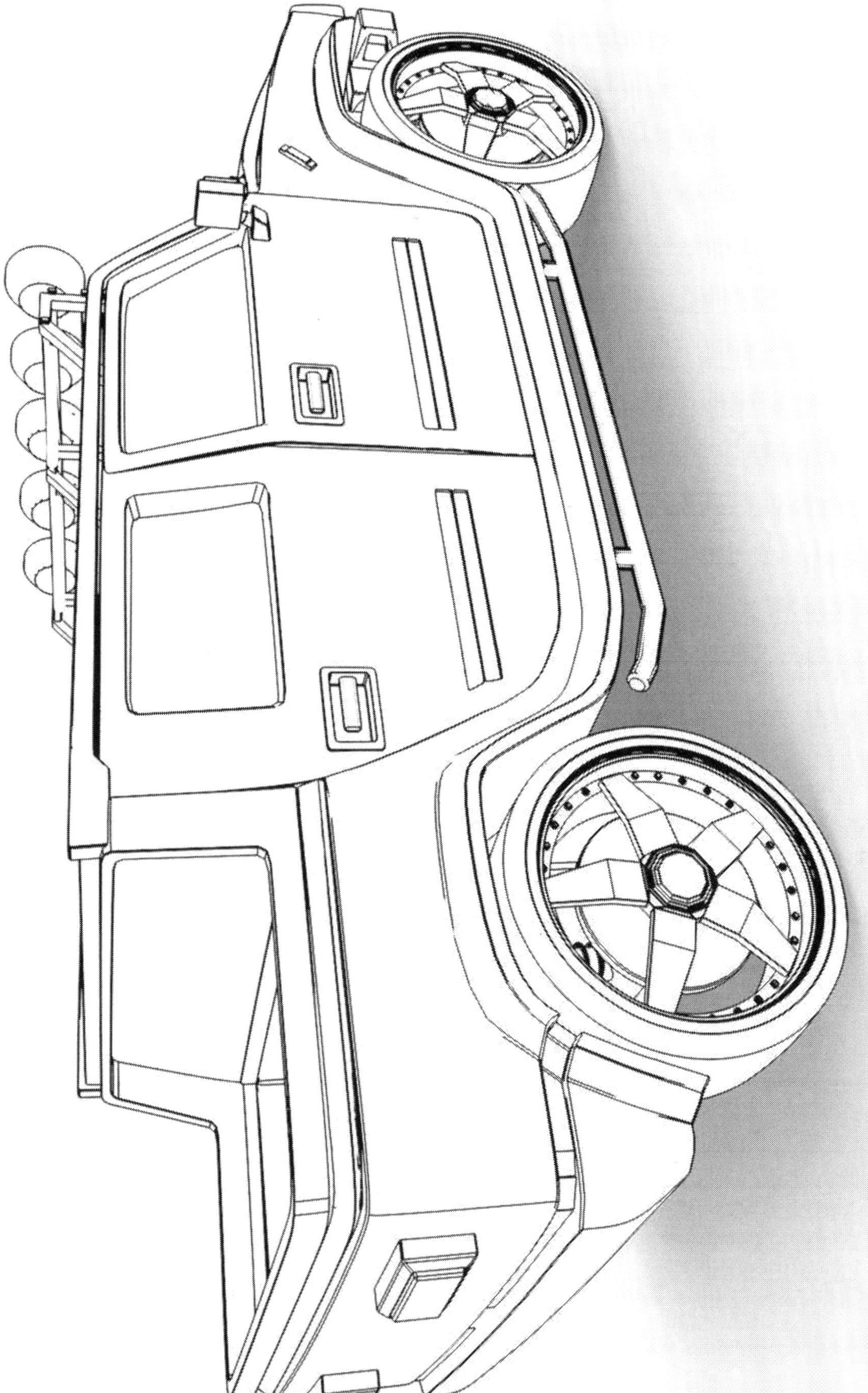

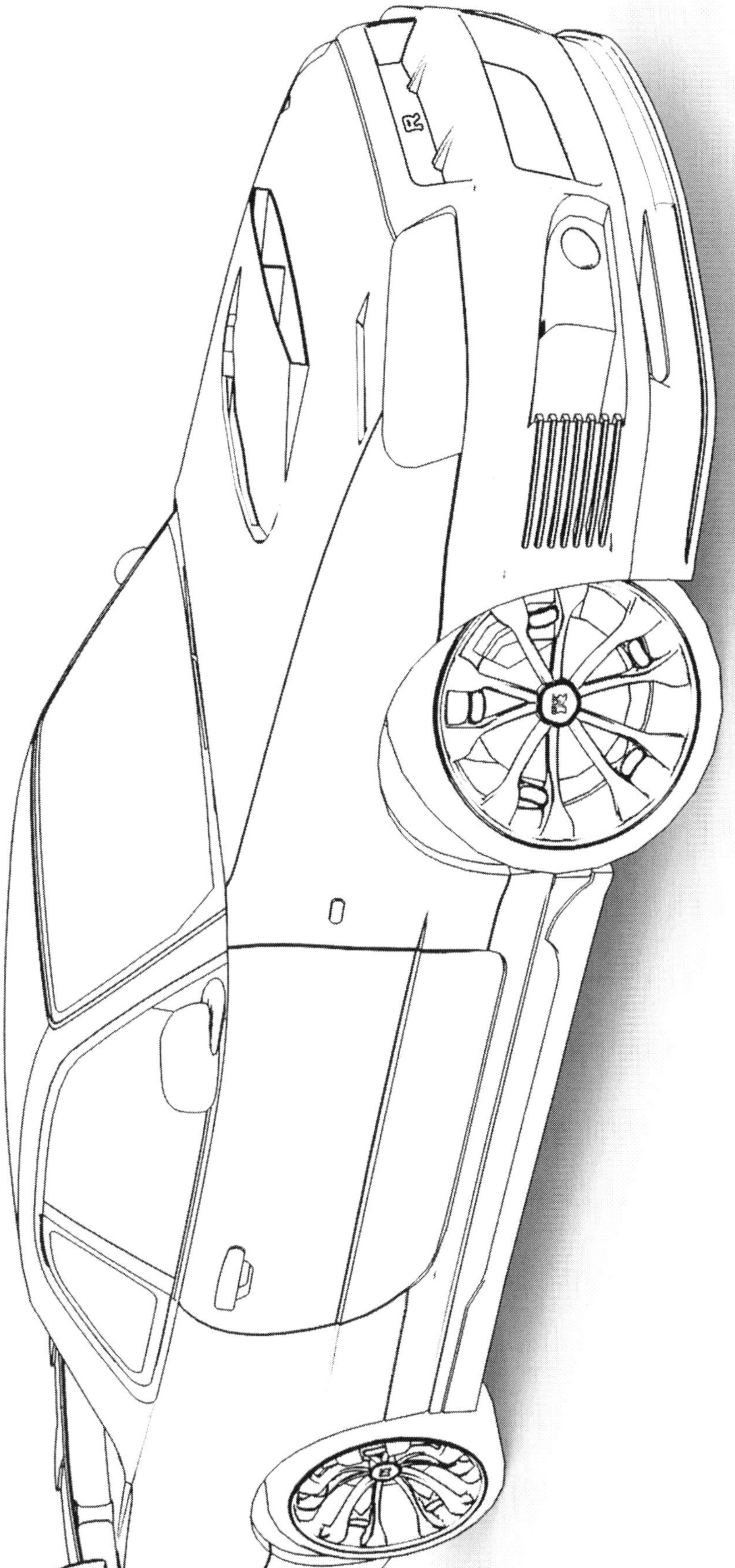

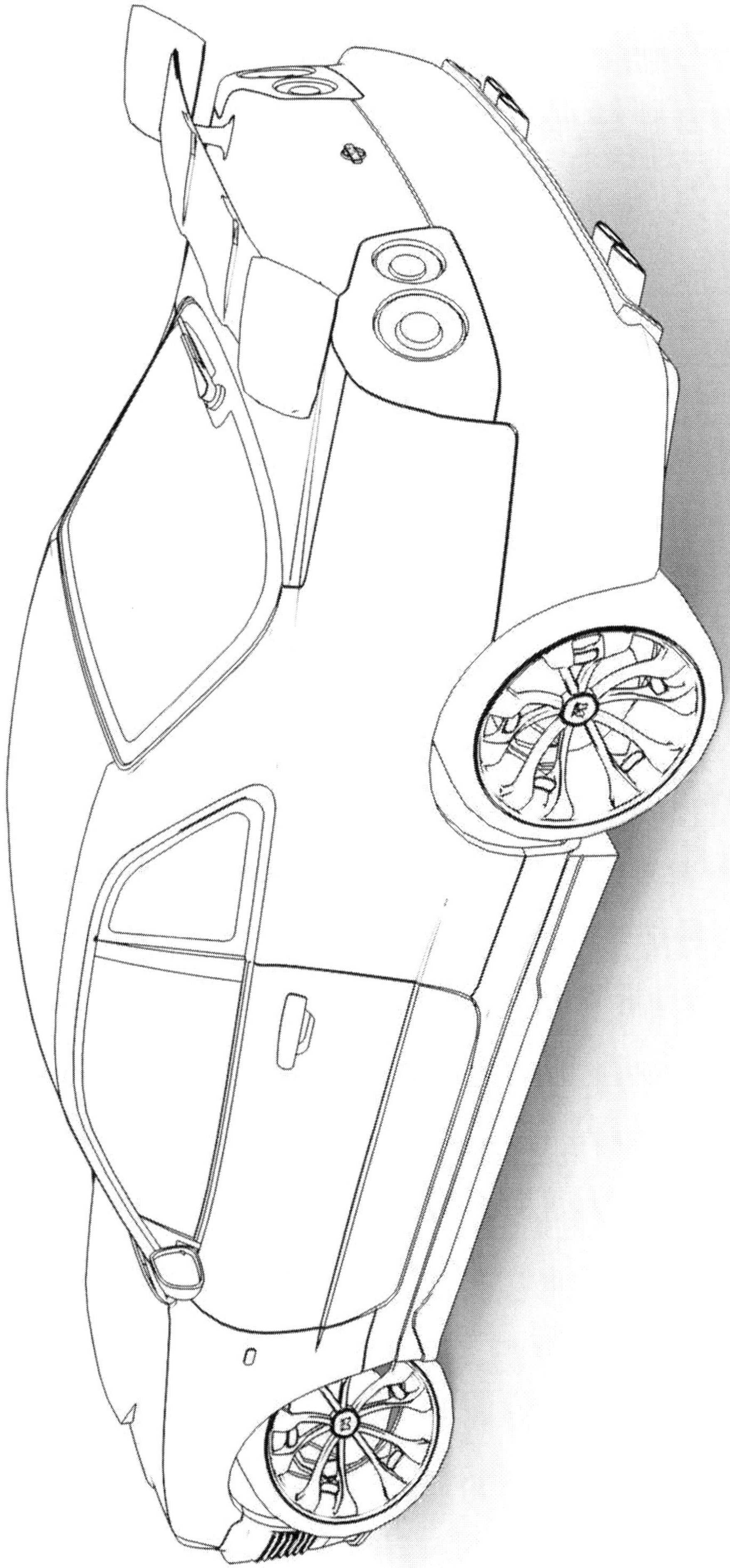

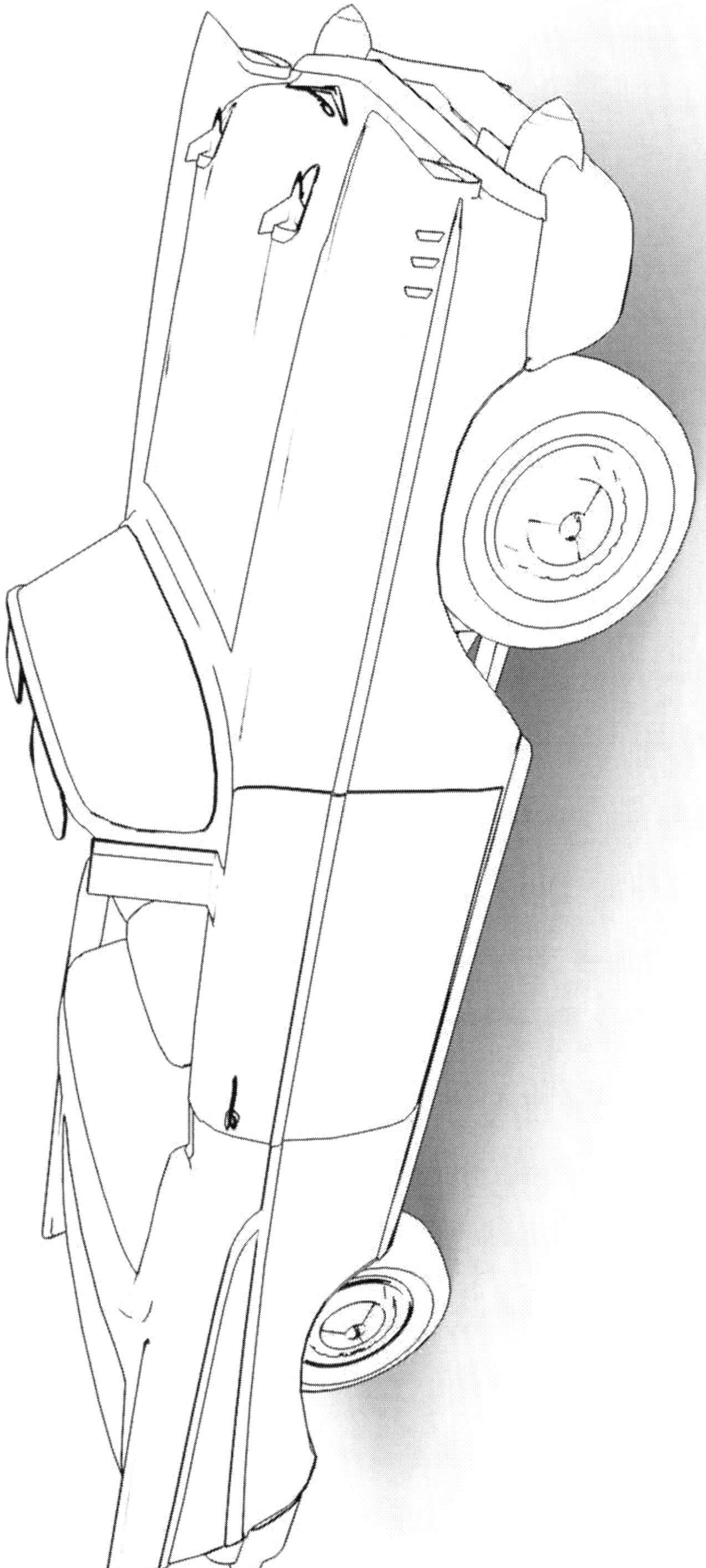

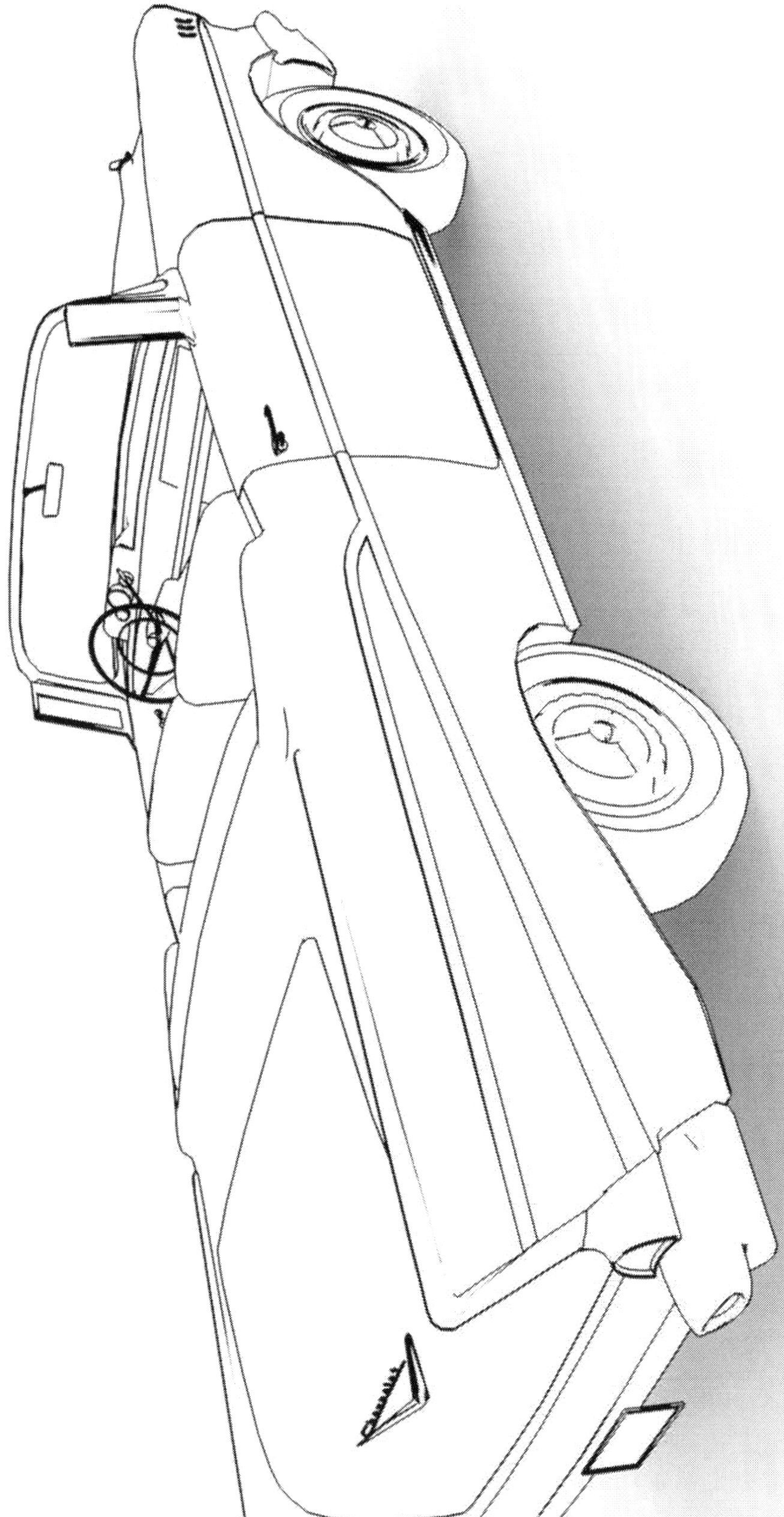

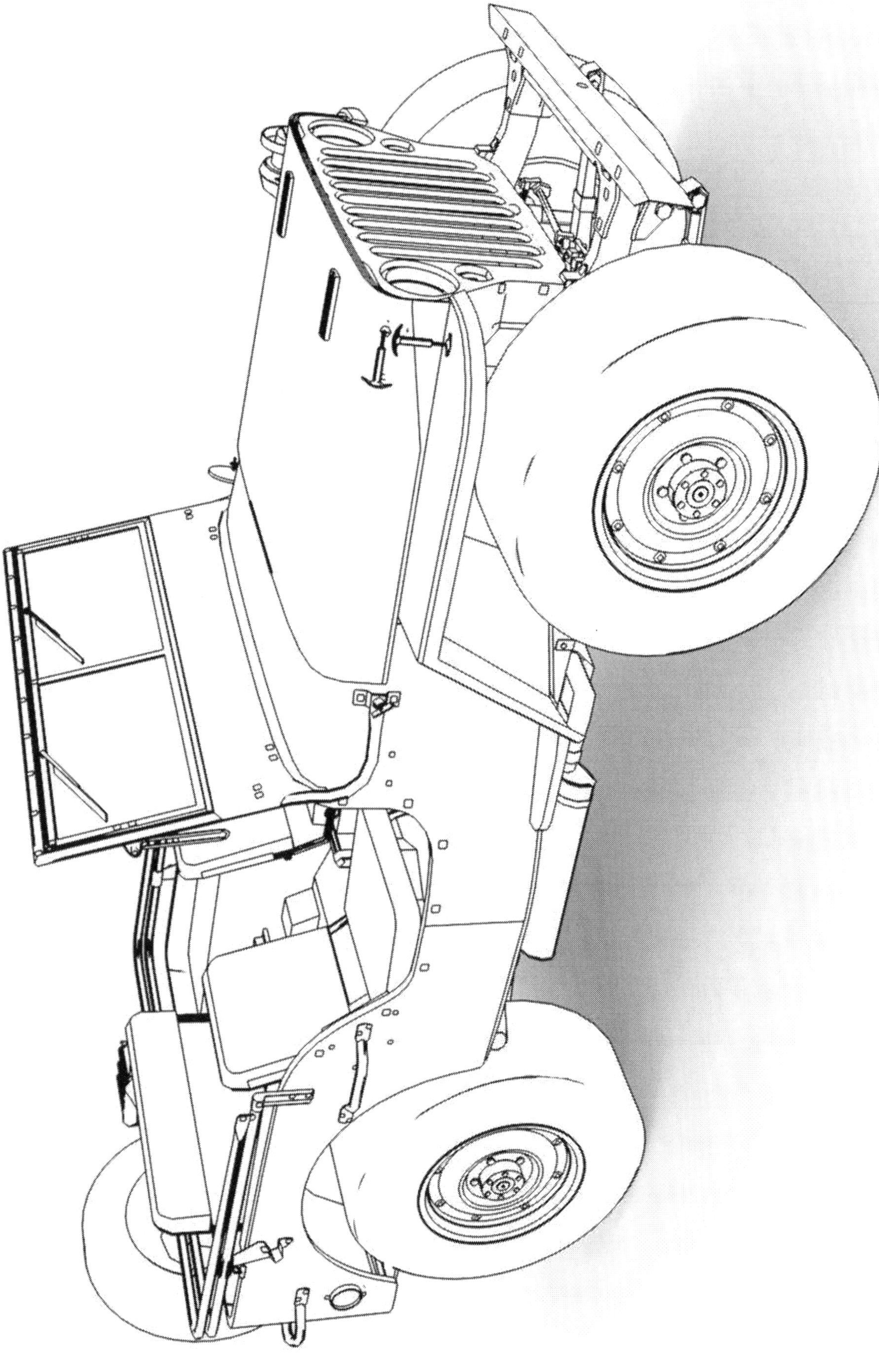

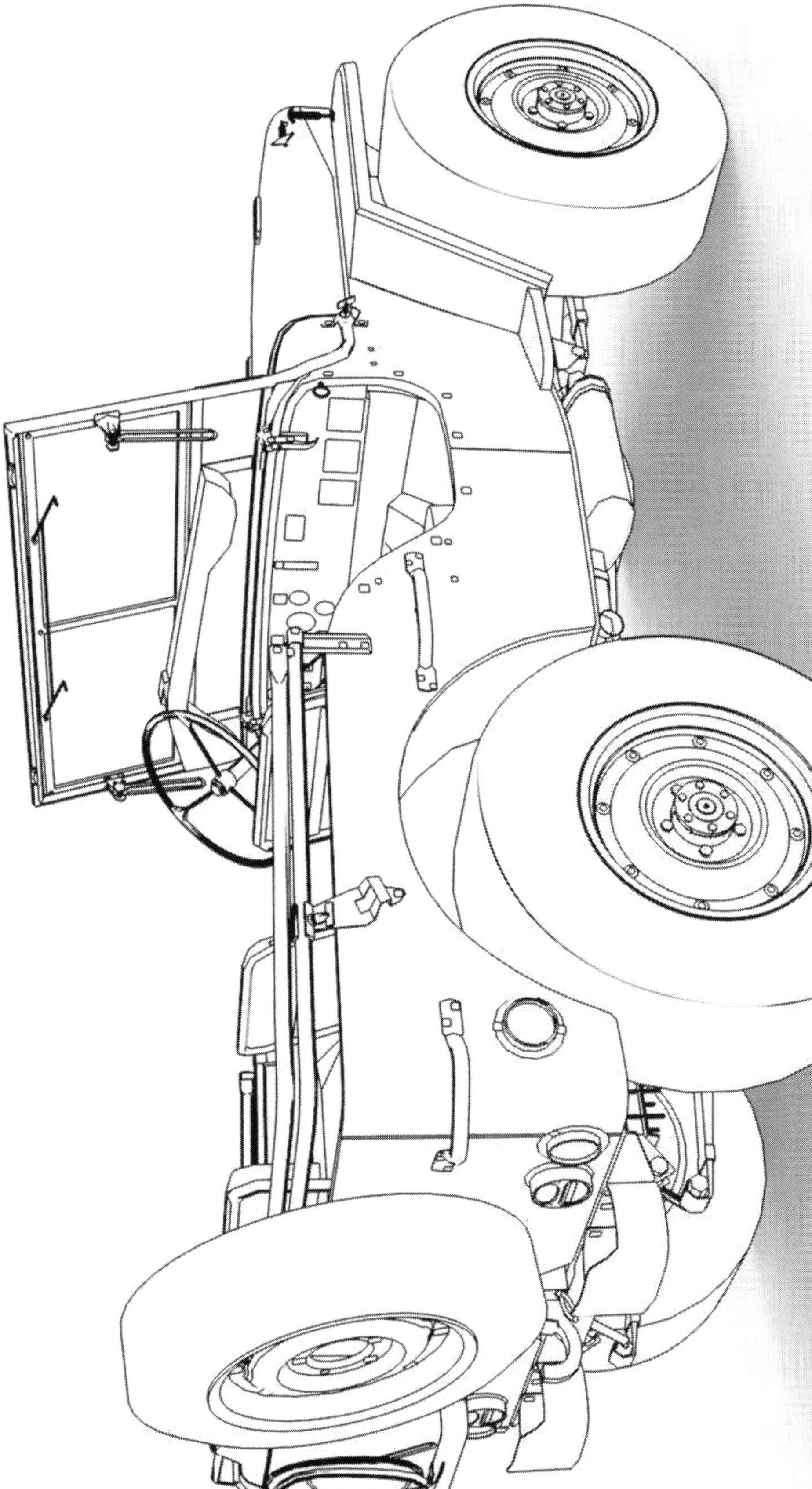

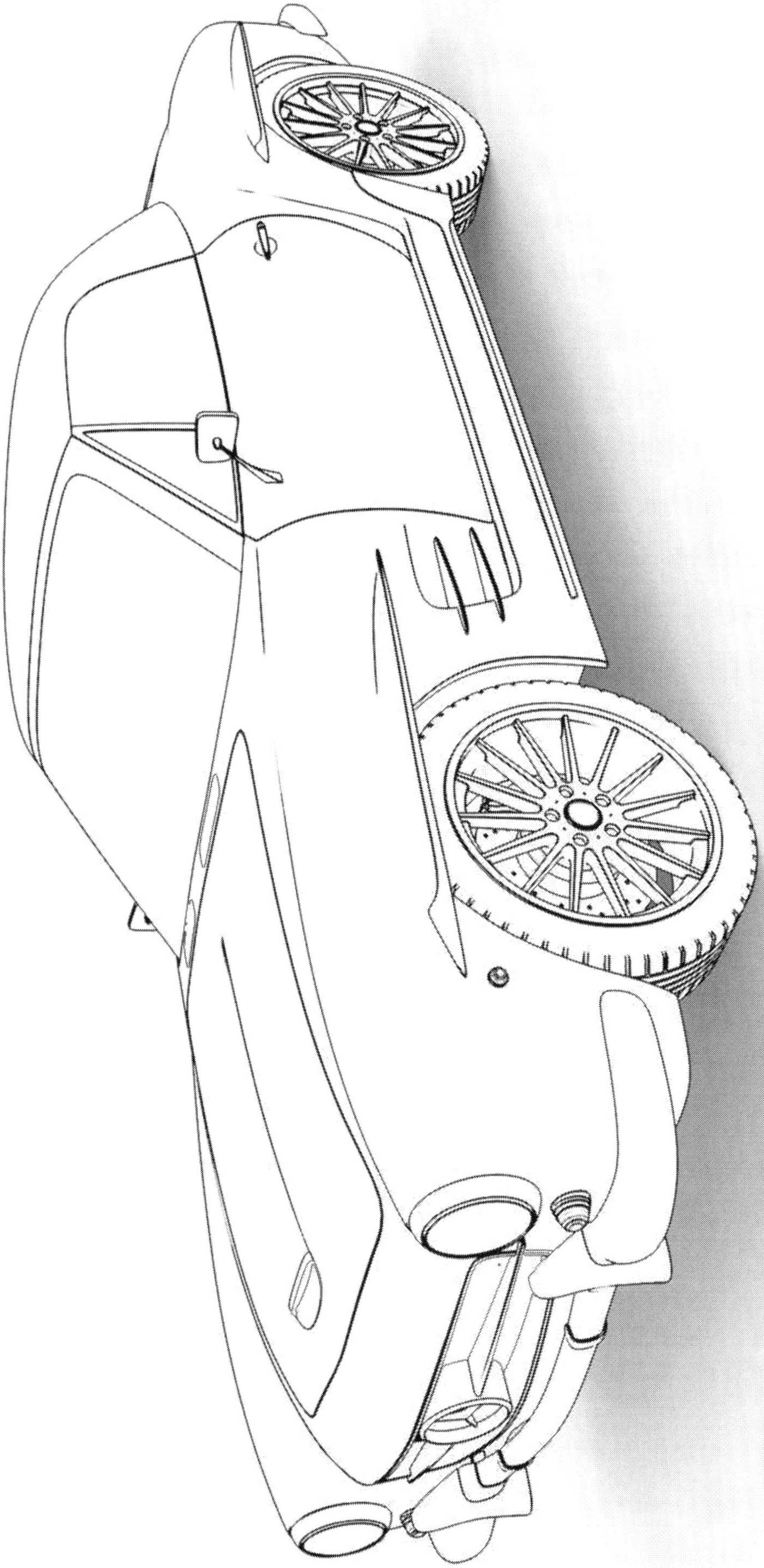

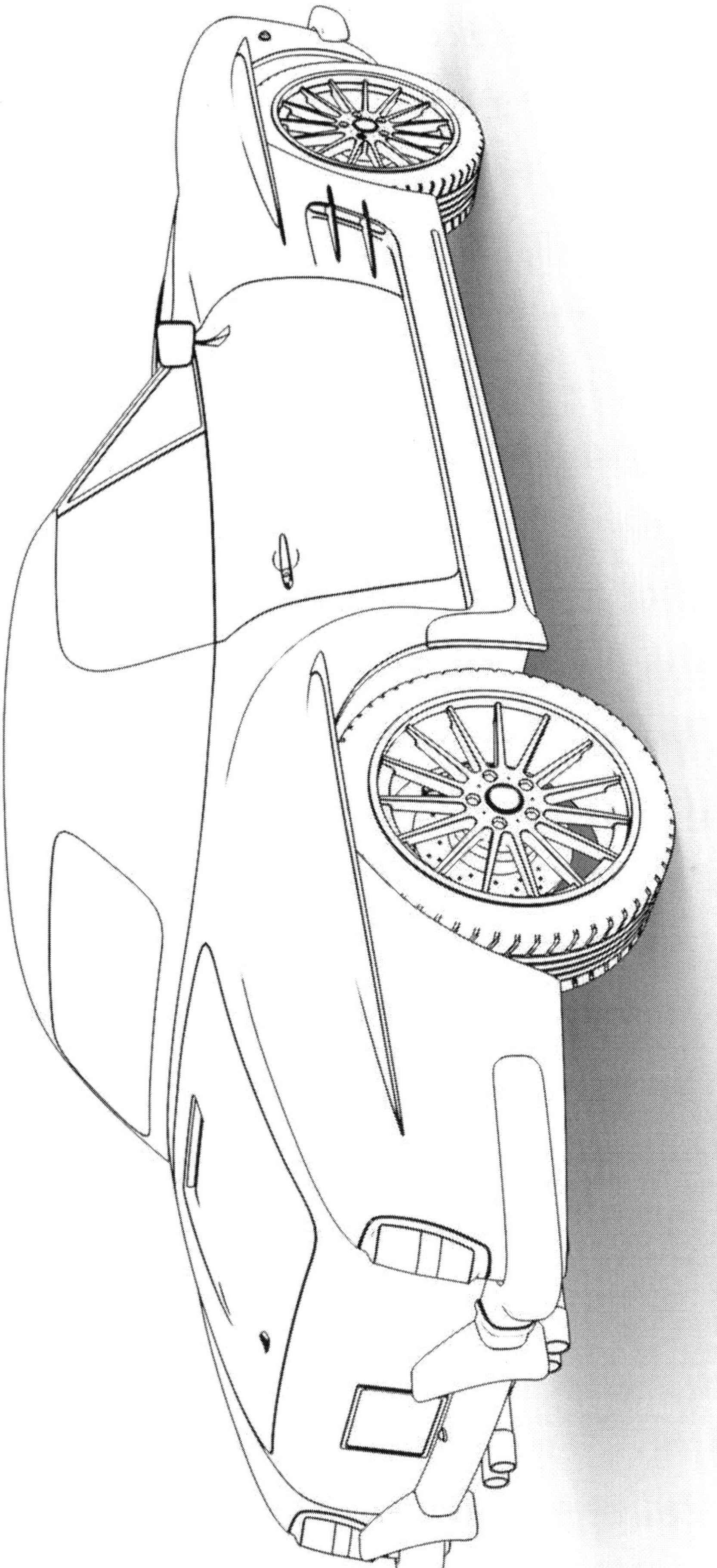

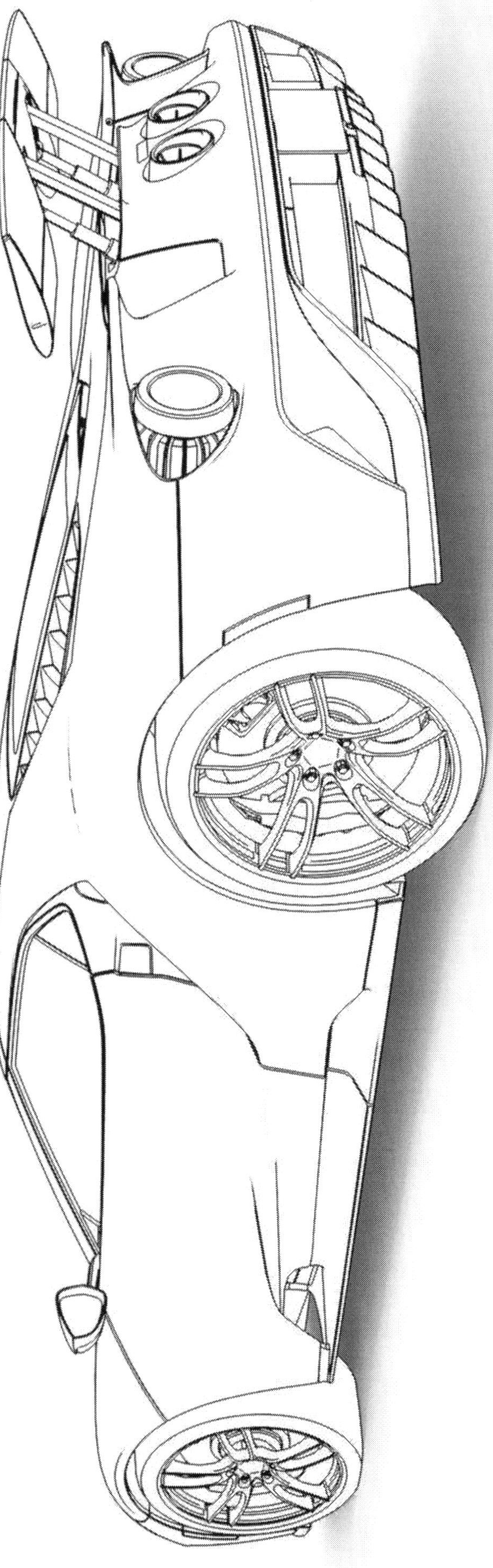

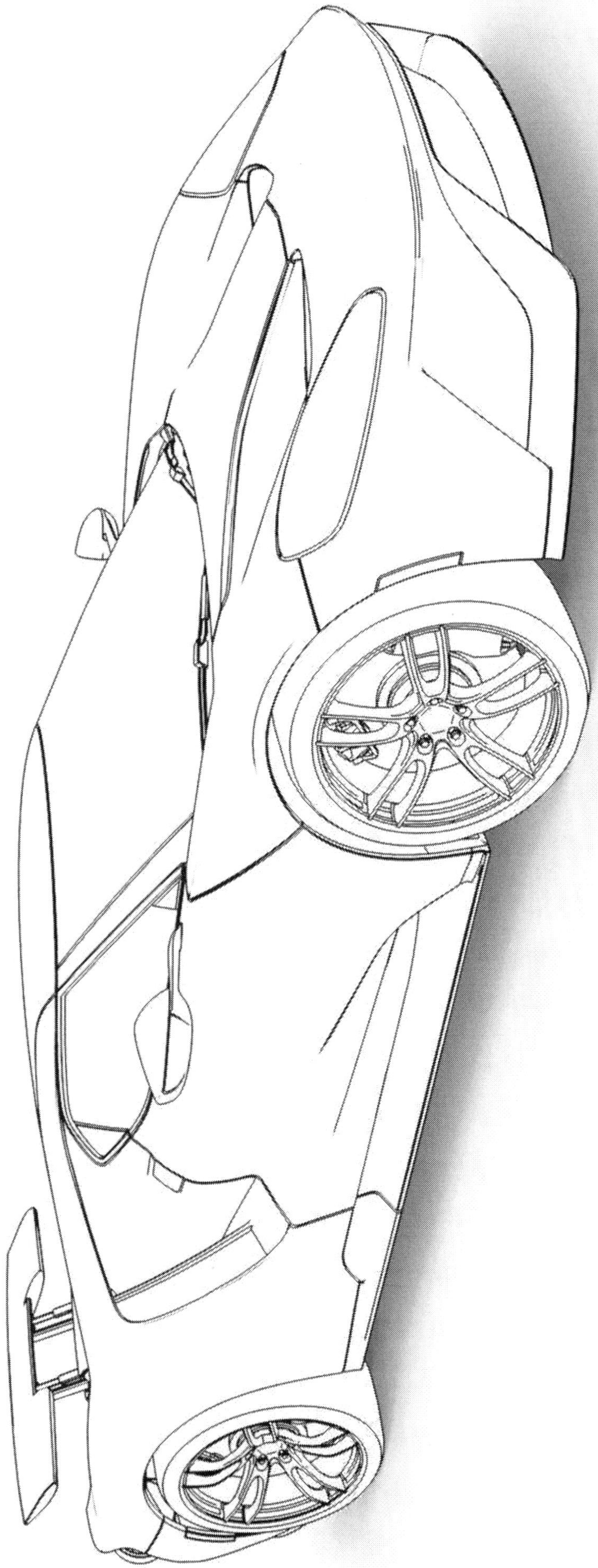

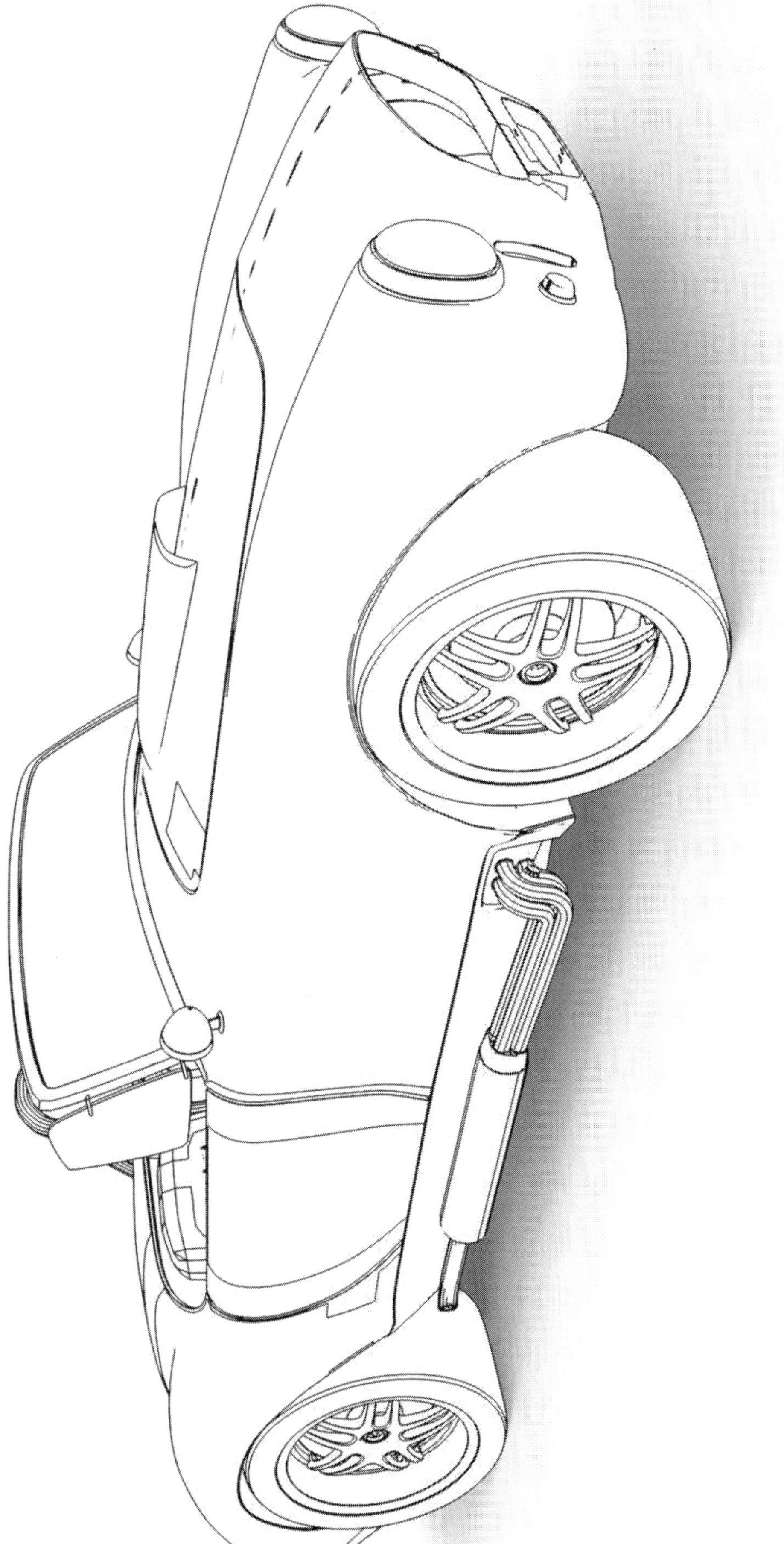

Printed in Poland
by Amazon Fulfillment
Poland Sp. z o.o., Wrocław

57472137R00045